PREFA

General Knowledge establish

of practically all serious assessment. Along these lines,

it is generally essential to ace general knowledge to try

the serious assessment to assist you with getting the

vocation of your fantasy. This handbook is a complete

reference for students of competitive examinations like

PSC, UPSC, railways, and other exams.

Disclaimer:

No part of this book may be reproduced, stored, in a retrieval system, or transmitted in any form or by any means without the prior written permission of the author and publisher except in accordance with the provisions of the Copyright, Designs and Patents Act 1988.

CONTENTS

GOVERNMENT OF INDIA

President: Smt Droupadi Murmu

Vice-President: Jagdeep Dhankhar

Current Cabinet Minister of India

Portfolio	Minister
Prime Minister Ministry of Personnel, Public Grievances and Pensions Department of Atomic Energy Department of Space	Narendra Modi
Minister of Defence	Rajnath Singh
Minister of Home Affairs Minister of Co-operation	Amit Shah
Minister of Finance Minister of Corporate Affairs	Nirmala Sitharaman
Minister of External Affairs	Subrahmanyam Jaishankar
Minister of Road Transport and Highways	Nitin Gadkari
Minister of Women and ChildDevelopment Minister of Minority Affairs	Smriti Zubin Irani
M inister of Commerce and Industry Minister of Consumer Affairs, Food and Public Distribution Minister of Textiles	Piyush Goyal
Minister of Law and Justice	Kiren Rijiju
Minister of Education Minister of Skill Development and Entrepreneurship	Dharmendra Pradhan
Minister of Agriculture & Farmers Welfare Minister of Rural Developement Minister of Panchayati Raj	Narendra Singh Tomar
Minister of Social Justice and Empowerment	Dr. Virendra K umar
Minister of Health and Family Welfare	Mansukh L. Mandaviya

Minister of Chemicals and Fertilizers	
Minister of Environment, Forest and Climate Change Minister of Labour and Employment	Bhupender Yadav
Minister of Jal Shakti	Gajendra Singh Shekhawat
Minister of Heavy Industries and Public Enterprises	Mahendra Nath Pandey
Minister of Parliamentary Affairs Minister of Coal Minister of Mines	Pralhad Joshi
Minister of Micro, Small and Medium Enterprises	Narayan Tatu Rane
Minister of Animal Husbandry, Dairying and Fisheries	Parshottam Rupala
Minister of Railways Minister of Communications Minister of Electronics and Information Technology	Ashwini Vaishnaw
Minister of Ports, Shipping and Waterways Minister of AYUSH	Sarbananda Sonowal
Minister of Rural Development Minister of Panchayati Raj	Giriraj Singh
MinisterofCivilAviation	Jyotiraditya Scindia
MinisterofSteel	Ramchandra Prasad Singh
Minister of Food Processing Industries	Pashupati Kumar Paras
Minister of Power Minister of New and Renewable Energy	Raj Kumar Singh
Minister of Petroleum and Natural Gas Minister of Housing and Urban Affairs	H ardeep Singh Puri
Minister of Culture Minister of Tourism Minister of Development of North Eastern Region	G. Kishan Reddy
Minister of Information and Broadcasting Minister of Youth Affairs and Sports	Anurag Thakur

Current Ministers of State (Independent Charge) of India

Portfolio	Minister
Minister of Statistics and Programme Implementation Minister of Planning Ministry of Corporate Affairs	Rao Inderjit Singh
Ministry of Science and Technology Ministry of Earth Sciences Minister of State in the Prime Minister's Office Miinistry of Personnel, Public Grievances and Pensions Department of Atomic Energy Department of Space	Jitendra Singh

Current Constitutional Head of India:

Office	Name
President	DroupadiMurmu
Vice President and ex-officio Chairperson of the Rajya	JagdeepDhankhar
Prime Minister	Narendra Modi
Chief Justice	Uday UmeshLalit
Speaker of the LokSabha	Om Birla
Chief ElectionCommissioner	Rajiv Kumar
Comptroller and Auditor General	GirishChandraMurmu
Chairperson of the Union Public Service Commission	Dr. Manoj Soni
Attorney Genera	R. Venkataramani

Current Bureaucrats of India:

Office	Name
National Security Advisor	Ajit Doval
Cabinet Secretary	Rajiv Gauba
Principal Secretary to the Prime Minister	Pramod Kumar Misra
Home Secretary	Ajay Kumar Bhalla
Finance Secretary	T.V. Somanathan
Defence Secretary	Ajay Kumar
Foreign Secretary	Vinay Mohan Kwatra
Law Secretary	Dr. Niten Chandra
Secretary General of the Lok Sabha	Utpal Kumar Singh
Secretary General of the Rajya Sabha	Pramod Chandra Mody
Secretary General of Supreme Court of India	Virendra Kumar Bansal
Chairperson of the Railway Board	Vinay Kumar Tripathi
Solicitor General	Tushar Mehta
Principal Scientific Adviser	Ajay K. Sood
Chief Economic Adviser	V Anantha Nageswaran

Current Head of Different Commission in India:

Office	Name
Chairperson of the National Human Rights Commission	ArunKumar Mishra
Chairperson of the National Commissionfor Minorities	Sardar Iqbal Singh Lalpura
Chairperson of the National Commissionfor Scheduled Castes	VijaySampla
Chairperson of the National Commissionfor Scheduled Tribes	Harsh Chouhan
Chairperson of the National Commissionfor Backward Classes	Bhagwan Lal Sahni
Chairperson of the National Commissionfor	Rekha Sharma
Chairperson of the National Commissionfor Protection of ChildRights	Priyank Kanungo
Chairperson of the Central Administrative Tribunal	L.Narasimha Reddy
Chairperson of the Cetral Vigilance Commission	Suresh N. Patel
Chairperson of the Central Information Commission	Yashvardhan Kumar Sinha
Chairperson of the Atomic Energy Commission	Kamlesh Nilkanth Vyas
Secretary of the Department ofSpace	S.Somanath
Chairperson of the UniversityGrants Commission	M.Jagadesh Kumar
Chairperson of the Competition Commission of India	Ashok Kumar Gupta
Chairperson of the Central Water Commission	Narendra Kumar
Director of the Space Applications Centre	Nilesh M Desai
Chairperson of the National Forest	B. N. Kirpal

INTERNATIONAL NEWS

1. COVID-19

Coronavirus is one of the significant pathogens that fundamentally focuses on the human respiratory framework. Past flare-ups of coronaviruses (CoVs) incorporate the severe acute respiratory syndrome (SARS)-CoV and the Middle East respiratory syndrome (MERS)-CoV, which have been recently described as operators that are an incredible public health threat. In late December 2019, a group of patients was admitted to the hospital with an underlying determination of pneumonia of an obscure etiology. Over 10 million people worldwide have tested positive for the novel coronavirus and that number is quickly growing. These patients were epidemiologically connected to the seafood and wet animal wholesale market in Wuhan, Hubei Province, China. As per W.H.O, coronaviruses belong to a group of RNA viruses that typically cause Upper Respiratory Infections. It causes diseases that range from the common cold to more severe ones such as (MERS)-CoV and (SARS)-CoV.

From December 18, 2019, through December 29, 2019, five patients were hospitalized with acute respiratory distress syndrome and one of these patients kicked the bucket. By January 2, 2020, 41 hospital patients had been distinguished as having research facility affirmed COVID-19 contamination, not exactly 50% of these patients had basic sicknesses, including diabetes, hypertension, and cardiovascular infection. These patients were dared to be contaminated in that hospital, likely because of nosocomial disease. As of January 22, 2020, a sum of 571 instances of the 2019-new coronavirus (COVID-19) was accounted for in 25 territories (regions and urban areas) in China. The China National Health Commission revealed the subtleties of the initial 17 passings up to January 22, 2020. On January 25, 2020, a sum of 1975 cases was affirmed to be tainted with the COVID-19 in territory China with an aggregate of 56 passings. Another report on January 24, 2020, evaluated the combined frequency in China to be 5502 cases. As of January 30, 2020, 7734 cases have been affirmed in China and 90 different cases have additionally been accounted for from various nations that incorporate Taiwan, Thailand, Vietnam, Malaysia, Nepal, Sri Lanka, Cambodia, Japan, Singapore, Republic of Korea, United Arab Emirates, United States, The Philippines, India, Australia, Canada, Finland, France, and Germany.

A COVID-19 vaccine is intended to provide acquired immunity against severe acute respiratory syndrome coronavirus 2 (SARS-CoV-2), the virus that causes COVID-19. Prior to the COVID-19 pandemic, an established body of knowledge existed about the structure and function of coronaviruses causing diseases like severe acute respiratory syndrome (SARS) and Middle East respiratory syndrome (MERS). This knowledge accelerated the development of various vaccine platforms during early 2020. The initial focus of SARS-CoV-2 vaccines was on preventing symptomatic, often severe illness. The COVID-19 vaccines are widely credited for their role in reducing the severity and death caused by COVID-19.

As of late-December 2021, more than 4.49 billion people had received one or more doses (8+ billion in total) in over 197 countries. The Oxford-AstraZeneca vaccine was the most widely used.

Several variants have been named by WHO and labelled as a variant of concern (VoC) or a variant of interest (VoI). Delta dominated and then eliminated earlier VoC from most jurisdictions. Omicron's immune escapeability may allow it to spread via breakthrough infections, which in turn may allow it to coexist with Delta, which more often infects the unvaccinated.

> **Variants of SARS-CoV-2**

Name	Lineage	Detected
Alpha	B.1.1.7	UK
Beta	B.1.351	South Africa
Delta	B.1.617.2	India

Gamma	P.1	Brazil
Lambda	C.37	Peru
Mu	B.1.621	Colombia
Omicron	B.1.1.529	Botswana

2. Monkeypox Outbreak:

Monkeypox is an infectious viral disease that can occur in humans and some other animals. Symptoms include fever, swollen lymph nodes, and a rash that forms blisters and then crusts over.The time from exposure to onset of symptoms ranges from five to twenty-one days. The duration of symptoms is typically two to four weeks. There may be mild symptoms, and it may occur without any symptoms being known. The classic presentation of fever and muscle pains, followed by swollen glands, with lesions all at the same stage, has not been found to be common to all outbreaks.Cases may be severe, especially in children, pregnant women or people with suppressed immune systems.

The disease is caused by the monkeypox virus, a zoonotic virus in the genus Orthopoxvirus. The variola virus, the causative agent of smallpox, is also in this genus. It may spread from infected animals by handling infected meat or via bites or scratches. Human-to-human transmission can occur through exposure to infected body fluids or contaminated objects, by small droplets, and possibly through the airborne route. People can spread the virus from the onset of symptoms until all the lesions have scabbed and fallen off; with some evidence of spread for more than a week after lesions have crusted. Diagnosis can be confirmed by testing a lesion for the virus's DNA.

There is no known cure. A study in 1988 found that the smallpox vaccine was around 85% protective in preventing infection in close contacts and in lessening the severity of the disease. A newer smallpox and monkeypox vaccine based on modified vaccinia Ankara has been approved, but with limited availability. Other measures include regular hand washing and avoiding sick people and animals. Antiviral drugs, cidofovir and tecovirimat, vaccinia immune globulin and the smallpox vaccine may be used during outbreaks. The illness is usually mild and most of those infected will recover within a few weeks without treatment. Estimates of the risk of death vary from 1% to 10%, although few deaths as a consequence of monkeypox have been recorded since 2017.

3. Sri Lankan economic crisis:

The Sri Lankan economic crisis is an ongoing crisis in the island-state of Sri Lanka that started in 2019. It is the country's worst economic crisis since its independence in 1948. It has led to unprecedented levels of inflation, near-depletion of foreign exchange reserves, shortages of medical supplies, and an increase in prices of basic commodities. The crisis is said to have begun due to multiple compounding factors like tax cuts, money creation, a nationwide policy to shift to organic or biological farming, the 2019 Sri Lanka Easter bombings, and the impact of the COVID-19 pandemic in Sri Lanka. The subsequent economic hardships resulted in the 2022 Sri Lankan protests.

Sri Lanka had been earmarked for sovereign default, as the remaining foreign exchange reserves of US$1.9 billion as of March 2022 would not be sufficient to pay the country's foreign debt obligations for 2022, with $4 billion to be repaid. An International Sovereign Bond repayment of $1 billion is due to be paid by the government in July 2022. Bloomberg reported that Sri Lanka had a total of $8.6 billion in repayments due in 2022, including both local debt and foreign debt. In April 2022, the Sri Lankan government announced that it was defaulting, making it the first sovereign default in Sri Lankan history since its independence in 1948 and the first state in the Asia-Pacific region to enter sovereign default in the 21st century. In June 2022, then Prime Minister Ranil Wickremesinghe said in parliament that the economy had collapsed, leaving it unable to pay for essentials. In September 2022, a United Nations report said that the economic crisis is a result of officials' impunity for human rights abuses and economic crimes.

4. Turkish currency and debt crisis

The 2018–2022 Turkish currency and debt crisis is an ongoing financial and economic crisis in Turkey. It is characterized by the Turkish lira (TRY) plunging in value, high inflation, rising borrowing costs, and correspondingly rising loan defaults. The crisis was caused by the Turkish economy's excessive current account deficit and large amounts of private foreign-currency denominated debt, in combination with President Recep Tayyip Erdoğan's increasing authoritarianism and his unorthodox ideas about interest rate policy. Some analysts also stress the leveraging effects of the geopolitical frictions with the United States. Following the detention of American pastor Andrew Brunson, who was confined of espionage charges after the failed 2016 Turkish coup d'état attempt, the Trump administration exerted pressure towards Turkey by imposing further sanctions. The economic sanctions therefore doubled the tariffs on Turkey, as imported steel rises up to 50% and on aluminum to 20%. As a result, Turkish steel was priced out of the US market, which previously amounted to 13% of Turkey's total steel exports.

While the crisis was prominent for waves of major depreciation of the currency, later stages were characterized by corporate debt defaults and finally by contraction of economic growth. With the inflation rate stuck in the double digits, stagflation ensued. The crisis ended a period of overheating economic growth under Erdoğan-led governments, built largely on a construction boom fueled by foreign borrowing, easy and cheap credit, and government spending.

After a period of modest recovery in 2020 and early 2021 amid the COVID-19 pandemic, the Turkish lira plunged following the replacement of Central Bank chief Naci Ağbal with Şahap Kavcıoğlu, who slashed interest rates from 19% to 14%. The lira lost 44% of its value in 2021 alone.

The economic crisis is believed to have caused a significant decline in Erdoğan's and AKP's popularity, which lost most of Turkey's biggest cities including Istanbul and Ankara in the 2019 local elections.

5. United Kingdom cost of living crisis:

The United Kingdom cost of living crisis is an ongoing event starting in 2021, in which prices for many essential goods in the United Kingdom began increasing faster than household incomes, resulting in a fall in real incomes. This is caused in part by a rise in inflation in the UK, in addition to the economic impact of global issues including the 2022 Russian invasion of Ukraine and COVID-19 pandemic. The UK's cost of living is the most affected of advanced economies. While all in the UK are affected by rising prices, it most substantially affects low-income persons. The British government has responded in various ways, such as by making provision for a £650 grant for each of the UK's lower income households.

6. European drought:

During the summer of 2022, parts of Europe experienced drought conditions exacerbated by heat waves. On 9 August, a senior European Commission researcher said it seems to be Europe's worst year in 500 years. A report from the Global Drought Observatory has confirmed this. The drought had serious consequences for hydropower generation and the cooling systems of nuclear power plants, as the drought reduced the amount of river water available for cooling. Agriculture in Europe was also negatively affected by the drought.

7. Food Crises:

2022 saw a rapid increase in food prices and shortages of food supplies around the world. The compounding crises in distinct parts of the world were caused by compounding geopolitical and economic crisis. The crises follow food security and economic crises during the COVID-19 pandemic.

Following the 2022 Russian-Ukraine war, the Food and Agriculture Organization, as well as other observers of the food commodities markets, warned of a collapse in food supply and price increases. Much of the concern is related to supply shortages of key commodity crops, such as wheat, corn, and oil seeds, which could cause price increases. The Russo-Ukraine war also led to fuel and associated fertilizer price increases, causing further food shortfalls and price increases.

Even before the invasion, food prices were already at record highs. As of February 2022, year-over-year food prices were up 20%, according to the Food and Agriculture Organization. The war further increased year-over-year prices another 40% in March. The compounding issues, including the Russian invasion of Ukraine, as well as climate-related crop failures, are expected to reverse global trends in reducing hunger and malnutrition.

Some regions, such as East Africa and Madagascar, were already experiencing drought and famine due to agricultural system failures and climate change, and the price increases are expected to make the situation worse. Even Global North countries that usually have secure food supplies, such as the UK and US, are beginning to experience the direct impacts of cost inflation due to food insecurity. Some analysts described the price increases as the worst since the 2007–2008 world food price crisis. Though initial international responses to the food crisis suggested that some suppliers or harvests may alleviate to global shortages and price increases (e.g. a proposed influx of grain from India), as of June 2022 no international efforts have been effective at alleviating prices.

8. Pakistan floods:

Since June 14, 2022, floods in Pakistan have killed 1,678 people. The floods were caused by heavier than usual monsoon rains and melting glaciers that followed a severe heat wave, all of which are linked to climate change. It is the world's deadliest flood since the 2017 South Asian floods and described as the worst in the country's history. On 25 August, Pakistan declared a state of emergency because of the flooding. The government of Pakistan has estimated losses worth US$40 billion from the flooding.The location   of   floods   are Balochistan, Gilgit-Baltistan, southern parts of Punjab, Sindh, Azad

Kashmir, Khyber Pakhtunkhwa.The causes of flood are Poor urban planning, Heavy monsoon rains, and climate change.

9. California wildfires:

The 2022 California wildfire season is an ongoing series of wildfires burning throughout the U.S. state of California. As of 21 September 2022, a total of 6,473 fires have been recorded, totaling approximately 365,140 acres (147,770 hectares) across the state. Wildfires have killed 9 people so far in California in 2022, have destroyed 772 structures, and damaged another 104. The 2022 season follows the 2020 and 2021 California wildfire seasons, which had the highest and second-highest (respectively) numbers of acres burned in the historical record.

A number of early-season wildfires helped raise concerns. In January 2022, the Colorado Fire in Monterey County became the first incident of the year in California, exhibiting "surreal fire behavior given the wet Oct and Dec". In February, the Airport Fire near Bishop Airport in Inyo County burned over 4,000 acres.

Drastic climatic and ecological conditions, including climate change and long-term drought, led to the anticipation of a potentially above-average wildfire season on the heels of two previous such seasons in 2020 and 2021. However, while the number of fires to date in 2022 is slightly above the 5-year average (6,465 fires versus 6,366 fires), the total acreage burned so far is well below the 5-year average; 365,140 acres have burned in 2022 thus far versus 1,712,797 acres burned by this time on average in the past five years (though that period includes several of California's most significant fire seasons). Peak fire season in California typically occurs in late summer and/or fall, and effectively ends when significant precipitation occurs across the state.

A number of significant wildfires have burned in California so far this year, including the destructive Oak Fire in Mariposa County, which burned over 180 structures, and the fatal McKinney Fire in Siskiyou County, which caused 4 fatalities. Major wildfires currently active include the Mosquito Fire in Placer and El Dorado counties, which has become California's largest wildfire of 2022, and the Fairview Fire in Riverside County.

Nobel Prizes and Laureates 2021		
Field	**Nobel Laureates**	**Contribution**
Physiology or Medicine	David Julius and Ardem Patapoutian	Discovery of receptors in the skin that sense heath & touch
Physics	Syukuro Manabe, Klaus Hasselmann and Giorgio Parisi	Understanding of Earth's climate change & other complex physical systems
Literature	Abdulrazak Gurnah	Covering the life of refugees and the effect of imperialism and its legacies on the lives of those who have been displaced
Chemistry	Benjamin List and David MacMillan	Development of asymmetric organocatalysis
Peace	Maria Ressa and Dmitry Muratov	Attempt to guard freedom of expression
Economics	David Card, Joshua Angrist and Guido Imbens	Completely reshaped empirical work in the economic sciences

SPORTS

INTERNATIONAL SPORTS	
Name	**Group**
American Cup	Yacht Racing
Ashes	Cricket
Benson and Hedges	Cricket
Canada Cup	Golf
Colombo Cup	Football
Corbitton Cup	Table Tennis (Women)
Davis Cup	Lawn Tennis
Derby	Horse Race
Grand National	Horse Streple, Chase Race
Jules Rimet Trophy	World Soccer Cup
King's Cup	Air Races
Merdeka Cup	Football
Ryder Cup	Golf
Swaythling Cup	Table Tennis (Men)
Thomas Cup	Badminton
U.Thant Cup	Tennis
Uber Cup	Badmintan (Women)
Walker Cup	Golf
Wightman Cup	Lawn Tennis
World Cup	Cricket, Hockey and Weightlifting
Reliance Cup	Cricket
Rothman's Trophy	Cricket
William's Cup	Basketball
European Champions Cup	Football
Eisenhower Cup	Golf
Essande Champions Cup	Hockey
Rene Frank Trophy	Hockey
Grand Prix	Table Tennis
Edgbaston Cup	Lawn Tennis
Grand Prix	Lawn Tennis

NATIONAL SPORTS	
Name	**Group**
Agarwal Cup	Badminton
Aga Khan Cup	Hockey
All India Women's Guru Nanak Championship	Hockey
Bandodkar Trophy	Football
Bangalore Blues Challenge Cup	Basketball
Barna-Bellack Cup	Table Tennis
Beighton Cup	Hockey
Bombay Gold Cup	Hockey
Burdwan Trophy	Weightlifting
Charminar Trophy	Atheletics
Chadha Cup	Badminton
Deodhar Trophy	Cricket
Duleep Trophy	Cricket
D.C.M Cup	Football
Durand Cup	Football
Dhyan Chand Trophy	Hockey
Dr. B.C.Roy Trophy	Football (Junior)
Ezra Cup	Polo
F.A.Cup	Football
G.D. Birla Trophy	Cricket
Ghulam Ahmed Trophy	Cricket
Gurmeet Trophy	Hockey
Guru Nanak Cup	Hockey
Gyanvati Devi Trophy	Hockey
Holker Trophy	Bridge
Irani Trophy	Football
I.F.A Shield	Football
Indira Gold Cup	Hockey
Jawaharlal Challenge	Air Racing

Jaswant Singh Trophy	Best Services Sportsman
Kuppuswamy Naidu Trophy	Hockey
Lady Rattan Tata Trophy	Hockey
MCC Trophy	Hockey
Moinuddaula Gold Cup	Hockey
Modi Gold Cup	Hockey
Narang Cup	Badminton
Nehru Trophy	Hockey
Nixon Gold Cup	Football
Obaid Ullah Gold Cup	Hockey
Prithi Singh Cup	Polo
Rani Jhansi Trophy	Cricket
Ranji Trophy	Cricket
Rangaswami Cup	Hockey
Ranjit Singh Gold Cup	Hockey
Rajendra Prasad Cup	Tennis
Ramanuja Trophy	Table Tennis
Rene Frank Trophy	Hockey
Rohinton Baria Trophy	Cricket
Rovers Cup	Football
Sanjay Gold Cup	Football
Santosh Trophy	Football
Sir Ashutosh Mukherjee	Football
Subrata Trophy	Football
Scindia Gold Cup	Hockey
Sahni Trophy	Hockey
Sheesh Mahal Trophy	Cricket
Tood Memorial Trophy	Football
Tommy Eman Gold Cup	Hockey
Vittal Trophy	Football
Vizzy Trophy	Cricket
Wellington Trophy	Rowing
Wills Trophy	Cricket

Sports Measurements

Badminton Courts: 44 ft. by 20 ft (doubles) 44 ft. by 17 ft. (singles) .
Boxing Ring: 12 ft. by 28 ft. Sq.
Cricket Pitch: 22 yards (distance)
Derby Course: 2.4 km
Football Field:
(a) Length : 100 - 120 yards , Breadth: 50 - 56 yards.
(b) Rugby : 100 yards by 75 yards
Hockey Ground: 100 yards by 55 to 60 yards
Lawn Tennis Court: 78 ft. by 36 ft. (double), 78 ft by 28 ft. (single)
Marathon Race: 26 miles, 385 yards
Polo Ground: 300 yards by 200 yards (if boarded)
Golf: Hole 44 inches in diameter.

Sports Terms

Badminton: Mixed doubles; Deuce; Drop; Smash; Let; Foot work; Setting.
Base Ball: Pitcher; Put out, Strike; Home; Bunt.
Billiards: Cue; Jigger; Pot; Break; In Baulk; In Off; Cannons.
Boxing: Upper cut; Round; Punch; Bout; Knock down; Hitting below the belt; Ring.
Bridge: Finesse; Dummy; Revoke; Grand Slam; Little Slam; No Trump; Rubber.
Chess: Bishop, Gambit; Checkmate; Stalemate.
Cricket: L.B.W.(leg before wicket); Creases, Popping-creases; Stumped; Bye; Leg-Bye; Googly; 'Hattrick; Maiden over; Drive; Bowling, Duck; Follow-on; No ball; Leg Break; Silly point; Cover point; Hit wicket; Late cut; Slip; Off-spinner, In-swing.
Football: Off Side; Block; Drop-kick; | Sticks; Off side; Roll in; Striking Circle; Penalty-kick (or goal kick); Corner-kick; Under-cutting; Dribble. Free-kick; Dribble; Thrown-in; Foul.
Golf: Boggy; Foursome; Stymic; Tee; Put; Hole; Niblic; Caddie; Links; The green; Bunker.
Horse racing: Jockey; Punter.
Hockey: Carried; Short Corner; Bully.
Polo: Bunker; Chukker; Mallet.

Tennis: Back hand drive; Volley; Smash; Half-volley; Deuce; Service; Let; Grand Slam.

Stadiums & Places Associated with Sports:

Name of Stadium	Sports	Place
Ambedkar Stadium	Football	Delhi
Aintree	Horse-race	England
Brabourne Stadium	Cricket	Mumbai
Black Heath	Rugby	London
Eden Garden	Cricket	Kolkata
Ferozshah Kotla	Cricket	Delhi
Shivajee Stadium	Hockey	Delhi
National Stadium	Hockey	Delhi
Nehru (Chepauk) Stadium	Cricket	Chennai
Ranjeet Stadium	Football	Kolkata
Indraprastha Stadium	Indoor Games	Delhi
Keenan Stadium	Cricket	Jamshedpur
Green Park Stadium	Cricket	Kanpur
White City	Dog-race	England
Wankhede Stadium	Cricket	Mumbai
Wembley Stadium	Football	London

Name of Playing Area of Different Games:

Name of Area	Related Sports
Alley	Bowling
Arena	Horse Riding
Board	Table Tennis
Course	Golf
Court	Lawn Tennis, Badminton, Netball, Hand ball, Volley ball, Squash, Kho-Kho, Kabaddi
Diamond	Baseball
Field	Polo, Football, Hockey
Rink	Ice Hockey
Ring	Boxing, Skating, Wrestling, Circus, Riding display
Pool	Swimming
Mat	Judo, Karate II
Track	Athletics
Vellodrum	Cycling

Number of Players in Some Sports:

Sports	No. of Players	Sports	No. of Players
Badminton	1 or 2	Rugby Football	15
Baseball	9	Hockey	11
Basketball	3	Lacrosse	12
Billiards	1	Netball	7
Boxing	1	Polo	4
Bridge	2	Table Tennis	1 or 2
Chess	1	Lawn Tennis	1 or 2
Cricket	11	Volleyball	6
Crocket	13/15	Water Polo	7
Football(Soccer)	11		

National Sports and Games of Some Countries:

Country	Sports/Games	Country	Sports/Games
Australia	Cricket	Scotland	Rugby football
Canada	Ice Hockey	Spain	Bull Fighting
England	Cricket and Rugby Football	USA	Baseball
India	Hockey	China	Table Tennis
Japan	Jujitsu	Malaysia	Badminton
Russia	Chess		

Olympic Games

Most importantly these games were held by the Greeks in 776 B.C. on Mount Olympus to pay tribute to the Greek God Zeus. Along these lines, the historical backdrop of the Olympic Games is around twenty 800 years of age. These games kept on being held at regular intervals until 394 A.D. At the point when these games were halted by an illustrious request of the head of Rome. The cutting edge Olympic Games which began in Athens in 1896, are the aftereffect of the commitment and devotion of a French teacher Baron Pierre de Coubertin and the primary Olympic gathering the advanced arrangement was held in 1896 in Athens, the Capital of Greece. From that point forward, they have been held at regular intervals, with the exception of breaks during universal wars. The Olympic flag is white color with five colored rings, each ling symbolic of a continent. Summer as well as winter Olympics are held in the same year.

Olympic Games: An Overview:

City	Country	Year	Opening ceremony	Closing ceremony
Athens	Greece	1896	6 April 1896	15 April 1896
Paris	France	1900	14 May 1900	28 October 1900
St. Louis	United States	1904	1 July 1904	23 November

				1904
London	United Kingdom	1908	27 April 1908	31 October 1908
Stockholm	Sweden	1912	5 May 1912	22 July 1912
Berlin	Germany	1916	Cancelled due to WWI	
Antwerp	Belgium	1920	20 April 1920	12 September 1920
Paris	France	1924	4 May 1924	27 July 1924
Amsterdam	Netherlands	1928	17 May 1928	12 August 1928
Los Angeles	United States	1932	30 July 1932	14 August 1932
Berlin	Germany	1936	1 August 1936	16 August 1936
Tokyo (Helsinki)	Japan	1940	Cancelled due to WWII	
London	United Kingdom	1944		
London	United Kingdom	1948	29 July 1948	14 August 1948
Helsinki	Finland	1952	19 July 1952	3 August 1952
Melbourne	Australia	1956	22 November	8 December 1956
Rome	Italy	1960	25 August 1960	11 September 1960
Tokyo	Japan	1964	10 October 1964	24 October 1964
Mexico City	Mexico	1968	12 October	27 October

			1968	1968
Munich	West Germany	1972	26 August 1972	11 September 1972
Montreal	Canada	1976	17 July 1976	1 August 1976
Moscow	Soviet Union	1980	19 July 1980	3 August 1980
Los Angeles	United States	1984	28 July 1984	12 August 1984
Seoul	South Korea	1988	17 September 1988	2 October 1988
Barcelona	Spain	1992	25 July 1992	9 August 1992
Atlanta	United States	1996	19 July 1996	4 August 1996
Sydney	Australia	2000	15 September 2000	1 October 2000
Athens	Greece	2004	13 August 2004	29 August 2004
Beijing	China	2008	8 August 2008	24 August 2008
London	United Kingdom	2012	27 July 2012	12 August 2012
Rio de Janeiro	Brazil	2016	5 August 2016	21 August 2016
Tokyo	Japan	2020(to be held)	23 Jul 2021	8 Aug 2021
Paris	France	2024	26 July 2024	11 August 2024 (to be

				held)
Los Angeles	USA	2028	21 July 2028	6 August 2028 (to be held)

Asian Games:

After the Second World War, the greater part of the Asian Countries picked up freedom. On the lines of Olympic Games, Asian Games were arranged at regular intervals. India facilitated the primary Asian Games in 1951.

Asian Game: An Overview

Year	Venues	Participating Countries	No. of Games	First Position
1951	New Delhi	11	6	Japan
1954	Manila	18	7	Japan
1958	Tokyo	20	13	Japan
1962	Jakarta	16	13	Japan
1966	Bangkok	18	14	Japan
1970	Bangkok	18	13	Japan
1974	Teheran	25	16	Japan
1978	Bangkok	25	19	Japan
1982	New Delhi	33	21	China
1986	Seoul	34	25	China
1990	Beijing	37	27	China
1994	Hiroshima	42	34	China
1998	Bangkok	41	36	China
2002	Busan	44	38	China
2006	Doha	46	43	China
2010	Guangzhou	45	43	China
2014	Incheon	45	42	China
2018	Jakarta and Palembang	45	46	China

2022	Hangzhou(China)	-	-	-
2026	Aichi-Nagoya(Japan)	-	-	-
2030	Doha(Qatar)	-	-	-
2034	Riyadh(Saudi Arabia)	-	-	-

Commonwealth Games

The Commonwealth Games are held at regular intervals.
The principal Commonwealth Games were held in 1930 at Hamilton (Canada).

Commonhealth Games: An Overview

Venues	Year	Participating Countries	Sports
Hamilton(Canada)	1930	11	6
London(U.K)	1934	16	6
Sydney(Australia)	1938	15	7
Auckland(New Zealand)	1950	12	7
Vancouver(Canada)	1954	24	9
Cardiff(U.K)	1958	35	9
Perth(Australia)	1962	35	9
Jamaika(West Indies)	1966	34	9
Edinburgh(U.K)	1070	42	9
Christchurch(New Zealand)	1974	39	9
Edmonton(Canada)	1978	48	10
Brisbane(Australia)	1982	47	10
Edinburgh(U.K)	1986	26	10
Auckland(New Zealand)	1990	55	10
Victoria(Canada)	1994	64	
Kuala Lumpur(Malaysia)	1998	70	16

Manchester(U.K)	2002	72	17
Melbourne (Australia)	2006	71	16
Delhi(India)	2010	71	17
Glasgow(Scotland)	2014	71	17
Gold Coast(Australia)	2018	71	19
Birmingham(England)	2022	72	20
State of Victoria(Australia)	2026	75	16

World Cup Cricket: An Overview

Venue	Winner	Runners-up	Year
U.K	West Indies	Australia	1975
U.K	West Indies	England	1979
U.K	India	West Indies	1983
India & Pakistan	Australia	England	1987
Australia	Pakistan	England	1992
India, Pakistan & Sri Lanka	Sri Lanka	Australia	1996
U.K	Australia	Pakistan	1999
South Africa	Australia	India	2003
West Indies	Australia	Sri Lanka	2007
India, Sri Lanka & Bangladesh	India	Sri Lanka	2011
Australia & New Zealand	Australia	New Zealand	2015
England & Wales	England	New Zealand	2019
India(to be held)	-	-	2023
India, Zimbabwe & Namibia(to be held)	-	-	2027
India & Bangladesh(to be held)	-	-	2031

World Cup Football: An Overview

Winner	Runners-up	Year
Uruguay	Argentina	1930
Italy	Czechoslovakia	1934
Italy	Hungary	1938
Uruguay	Brazil	1950
West Germany	Hungary	1954
Brazil	Sweden	1958
Brazil	Czechoslovakia	1962
England	West Germany	1966
Brazil	Italy	1970
West Germany	Poland	1974
Argentina	Holland	1978
Italy	West Germany	1982
Argentina	West Germany	1986
West Germany	Argentina	1990
Brazil	Italy	1994
France	Brazil	1998
Brazil	Germany	2002
Italy	France	2006
Spain	Netherlands	2010
Germany	Argentina	2014
France	Croatia	2018
Qatar(place to be held)	-	2022

UNITED NATION ORGANIZATION

Origin: UN Charter was signed by 50 members on June 26, 1945. It formally appeared on October 24,1945.

UN Charter: The charter is the Constitution of the UNO and contains its aims and objectives and rules and regulations for its functioning.

Aims and Objectives: Security, welfare and human rights.

Headquarters: New York

Flag: The banner is light blue in shading and decorated in white, in its middle is

the UN image a polar guide of the world grasped by twin olive branches open at the top.

Official Languages: English, French, Chinese, Russian, Arabic and Spanish. However, working languages are English & French only.

Secretary General of the U.N.O.

Name	Country	Tenure
Trygve Lie	Norway	(1946-53)
Dog Hznmarsk joeld	Sweden	(1953-61)
U. Thant	Myanmar	(1961-71)
Kurt Waldheim	Austria	(1971-81)
Javier Perez de Cuellar	Peru	(1981-91)
Dr. Boutros Ghali	Egypt	(1992-96)
Kofi Annan	Ghana	(1997-2006)
Ban Ki-moon	South Korea	(2007 -2016)
António Guterres	Portugal	(1 January 2017 - Present)

Main Organs of the UNO:

There are six main organs:

(1) General Assembly

(2) Security Council

(3) Economic and Social Council

(4) Trusteeship Council

(5) International Court of Justice

(6) Secretariat

(1) General Assembly: It consists of a representative of all members of the UN. Each member country has only one vote.It meets once per year and passes the UN spending plan.

(2) Security Council: It is the Executive body of the UN and is predominantly liable for keeping up international peace and security. It has 15 members, 5 of which (USA, UK, France, Russia and QIina) are permanent members. The 10 non-permanent members are elected by General Assembly for two-year term and are not qualified for guaranteed re-appointment.

(3) Economic and Social Council: It has 54 members elected by General Assembly.

(4) Trusteeship Council: It takes care of the interest of the people in territories not yet free and leads them towards self-government.

(5) International Court of Justice: It has 15 judges, no two of whom may be nationals of the same state. They are elected by General Assembly and Security Council for a term of 9 years. The Court elects its President and Vice-President for a 3 year term.

OTHER IMPORTANT ALLIANCES/ BODIES OF THE WORLD

Commonwealth of Nations: It is an important international body founded in Great Britain in 1931. It is a free association of 53 sovereign independent States formerly under British rule.

European Union (E.U.): It is the new name of the European Economic community (EEC) or European Common Market (ECM). Now a union of 27 European Nations. Members are: France, Germany, the Netherlands, Belgium, Italy, Luxembourg, Britain, Ireland, Denmark, Greece, Spain, Portugal, Austria, Finland, Sweden, Cyprus, Czech Republic, Estonia, hungary, Latvia, Lithuania, Malta, Poand, Slovakia, Slovania, Romania and Bulgaria. It is world's biggest and richest bloc.

Interpol: It is the popular name of the International Criminal Police Organization (ICPO). It has got 176 member countries. It was established in 1923.

International organizations, Headquarters and Year of Establishment

International organizations	Headquarters	Year of Establishment
United Nations Organizations (U.N.O.)	New York	1945
International Monetary Fund (I.M.F)	Washington	1945
World Health Organization (W.H.O.)	Geneva	1948
Food & Agricultural Organization (FAO)	Rome	1943
International Labour Organization (ILO)	Geneva	1919
UNESCO	Paris	1946
International Telecommunication Union (ITO)	Geneva	1947
International Maritime Organization (IMO)	London	1948
World Meteorological Organization (WMO)	Geneva	1951
International Atomic Energy Agency (IAEA)	Vienna	1957
International Court of Justice	The Hague	-
Universal Postal Union (UPU)	Berne	1874
International Finance Corporation (IFC)	Washington	1956
UNICEF	New York	1946
United Nation Development Programme (UNDP)	New York	-

International Civil Aviation Organization (ICAO)	Montreal	1947
UNIDO	Vienna	1967
World Trade Organization (WTO)	Geneva	1995
Arab League	Tunis	1945
International Development Association (IDA)	Washington D.C.	1960
World Intellectual Property Organization (WIPO)	Geneva	1967
Organization of Islamic Conference (OIC)	Mecca	1971
Asian Development Bank (ADB)	Manila	1966
North Atlantic Treaty Organization (NATO)	Brussels	1949
Association of South East Asian Nations (ASEAN)	Jakarta	1967
International Bank for Reconstruction and Development (IBRD)	Washington D.C.	1946
Red Cross	Geneva	1863
Interpol	Paris	1923
European Union	Geneva	1957
Commonwealth of Nations	London	1931

Amnesty International: It is known as worldwide human rights organizations. It was established on 28th May, 1961. It won the Nobel prize for Peace in 1977. Headquarters in London.

World Trade Organization (W.T.O.): The new world Trade Organization, which replaces the General Agreement on Tariffs and Trade (GATT), came into effect from January l, 1995 with the backing of at least 85 founding members, including India. The WTO presently comes as the third financial mainstay of overall measurements alongside the World Bank and International Monetary Fund.

Non-Aligned Movement (NAM): It is a group of 118 mostly developing countries. The principles of non-alignment were defined in the Bandung (Indonesia). The first NAM Conference was held at Belgrade in 1961. The basic thrust of the movement is in favor of peace, disarmament, development, independence, eradication of poverty and illiteracy.

ASEAN (Association of South East Asian Nation): It was established in 1967. The objectives of ASEAN are to promote active collaboration and mutual assistance in the economic, social, cultural, administrative and scientific: field to accelerate economic graft, social progress and cultural development in the region and promote regional peace and stability. Member Countries: Indonesia, Malaysia, Singapore, Thailand, Brunai, Philippines, Vietnam, Laos, and Myanmar. Headquarters: Jakarta (Indonesia).

North Atlantic Treaty Organization (NATO):
The treaty was signed at Washington April 4, 1949, by the Foreign of Belgium, Canada, Denmark, France, Iceland, Italy, Luxembourg, Netherlands, Irelands, Norway, Portugal, UK and USA. Greece, Turkey, German, Spain joined later. Poland, Hungary and Czech Republic were added on March 19, 1999. Romania, Bulgaria, Slovakia, Lithuania, Slovenia, Latvia and Estonia joined NATO April 2, 2004.

South Asian Association for Regional Cooperation (SAARC):
Member States: India, Bangladesh, Pakistan, Sri Lanka, Bhutan, Nepal, Maldives and Afghanistan. A permanent Secretariat of the SAARC has been set up at Kathmandu in Nepal. The first SAARC submit was held in Dhaka (Bangladesh) on December 1985.

Asian Development Bank (ADB): It was established in 1966. It is the Asian counterpart of the American Development Bank and African Development Bank. The headquarters of ADB is situated at Manila. It helps promote intra-regional trade.

Organization of Petroleum Exporting Countries (OPEC): It was established in 1973. It has 13 members with its headquarters in Vienna (Austria). OPEC countries supply around 85% of the world oil products

WORLD

Population: According to the United Nations Population Fund estimates, world population reached 7.3 billion in mid-2015, the growth rate being 1.1% while birth and death rates were at 20.1 and 8.2 per thousand population, respectively. China and India each has more than a billion people (China: 1.4 billion; India 1.3 billion). The United States has the third largest population (328 million) followed by Indonesia (267 million) and Brazil (212 million).

Most Populous Country: China is the most populous country in the world with a massive share of the world's population nearly 19 percent.

Least Populous Country: The independent state with the smallest populaüon is the Vatican City or the Holy See.

Most Densely Populated Country: The most densely populated country in the world is Monaco.

Number of Countries: The world comprises of 195 sovereign states, that includes 193 members of the United Nations and two non members, viz., Taiwan and Vatican City. Other than this, there are 72 dependent areas and other entities.

Largest Country: The country with the largest area is Russia, with a total area of 1,70,75,000 sq. km., or 11.5 per cent of the world's total land area. It is 70 times larger than the U.K.

Smallest Country: The smallest independent country in the world is the State of the Vatican city or the Holy See, which was made as an enclave within the city of Rome, Italy on February 11, 1929. The enclave has an area of 0.44 sq. km.

Smallest Republic: The world's smallest republic is Nauru, less than one degree south of the equator in the Central Pacific, which became independent on January 31, 1968. It has an area of 21 sq. km.

Most Populous urban agglomeration: Tokyo with a population of 36.9 million was the most populous urban agglqmeration.

Largest City: The world's largest city, in the area, is Jiuquan Gansu, China, which has an area of 1,67,996 square kilometer.

International Sobriquets

China's Sorrow	Hwang-Ho
City of Dreaming Spires	Oxford
County of Rising Sun	Japan
Britain of the South	New Zealand
City of Skyscrapers	New York
City of Golden Gate	San Francisco, U.S.A
City of Seven Hills	Rome, Italy
City of Magnificent Distances	Washington D.C
Cockpit of Europe	Belgium
Dark Continent	Africa
Emerald Island	Ireland
Empire City	New York
Forbidden City	Lhasa, Tibet
Great White Way	Broadway, New York, U.S.A
Gift of Nile	Egypt
Garden of England	Kent
Granite City	Aberdeen, Scotland
Herring Pond	Atlantic Ocean
Holy Land	Palestine
Hermit Kingdom	Korea
Island Continent	Australia
Island of Pearls	Bahrain
Island of Cloves	Zanzibar

WORLD HISTORY
Different Ages

Ice Age: Period, starting from 10,00,000 years back in which a progression of ice tops secured the vast majority of the northern pieces of the earth.

Stone Age: Period, in which men utilized devices and weapons made of stone. It started around 1,00,000 years prior.

Bronze Age: Period, when individuals utilized bronze apparatuses; period from 3,000 to 1,000 B.C.

Iron Age: Period, when people previously utilized iron instruments and weapons. It started at around 1,200 BC and lasted for 1,000 years.

Augustine Age: It alludes to the rule of the Emperor Augustus; 27 BC to 14 BC in Latin History.

Dim Age: Period, from the fall of Rome in 476 AD until 1000 AD.

Middle Age: Period, between ancient times and the modern period often given as between the fall of Roman Empire in the 5th century and the Renaissance in the 15th.

Elizabethan Age: Period of the primitive framework in Europe from 700 to 1400 AD.

Machine Age: Name given to the time of industrialization in Britain, started in 1750.

Age of Reason: The eighteenth century, when philosophy was making progress in Europe.

Victorian Age: Period, when Queen Victoria ruled, i.e., 1837-1901. It was a time of technological progress and public morality.

Nuclear Age: Period since the blast of the first atom bomb at Almogordo, New Mexico on July 16, 1945.

Development of Civilisation

The First Phase: The first phase start of the civilisation Neolithic Revolution, started when settled in the towns and turned into a rancher.

The Second Phase: The stage was when writing started. This occurred in the early Bronze Age (3200 to 2000 B.C.). Writing first created in southern Mesopotamia and in southwest Iran.

The Third Phase: The third started when Summerian city-states created. It occurred between 3100 to 2570 B.C.

The Fourth Phase: The fourth was that of the setting up of realms. The Summerian city states were joined into an incredible realm in 2370 B.C. by Sargon of Agade. The peak of this stage was the point at which the Persian realm, writing first.

The Fifth Phase: In this stage, civilisation moved from Asia to Mediterranean where it stayed for the 1000 years. There were city states Greece. During this stage, there two other significant impacts civilisation (I) that of Confucius (ii) of Buddha. Confucius, the Chinese rationalist, gave speculations which molded the political association of China numerous hundreds of years. Likewise, the lessons of Buddha practiced a ground-breaking impact on the civilisation of Indian subcontinent. The Indian Empire declined after death of King Ashoka (232 B.C.). Chinese Empire declined after the demise of the ruler Wu Ti. At that point showed up the renowned Roman domain when King Rumulus established Rome. It reached a conclusion in 476 A.D. Going through the Middle Age civilisation entered the cutting edge period. Numerous developments helped the improvement of civilisation.

Important Historical Dates of the World

B.C.
776: First Olympic Games in Greece
323:Alexander died at Babylone
221: Great Wall of China finished
4: Birth of Jesus
A.D.
30: Crucifixion of Jesus Christ

570: Birth of Prophet Mohammed at Mecca

622: Hizari era began, Hazrat Mohammad went from Macca to Madina

1453:Renaissance in Europe 1492. Columbus discovered America

1498: Sea-route to India discovered (Vasco Da Garna)

1668: Autocratic rule of Stuarts ended, and the Parliamentary rule started in England

1775: Announcement of American Independence (4th July)

1789: French revolution

1804-25: Industrial Revolution in England

1815: Battle of Waterloo

1865: Abraham Lincoln killed

1896: Olympic Games began in Athens

1904: Russia-Japan war
1914-18: World war I
1920: Revolution in Russia, the Czar killed.
1933: Hitler emerge as the Chancellor of Germany
1939-45: World War II

1945: First Atom Bomb dropped on Hiroshima (Aug. 6)and Nagasaki (Aug.9).

1948: Independence of Burma (4th January), Jews declared State of Israel in Palestine

1953: Mt. Everest conquered by Edmund Hillary and Tenzing Norgay.
1957: Artificial satellites (Sputniks I and II) launched by Russia.

1963: American president John F. Kennedy killed.

1969: American astronauts land on moon.

1975: Everest conquered by first woman Mrs. Juniko Tabei; Coup in Bangladesh Sheikh Mujib killed.

1976: Unification of Vietnams; Death of Mr. Mao-tse Tung

1977: America makes neutron bomb.

1997: NASA spacecraft (Path finder) landed on Mars

1998: Pakistan conducts Nuclear (Mav 28).

1999 : China launched Shenzhou in space an unmanned spacecraft .

2000 : George Bush elected President of USA (Dec 16).

2002: The 11th SAARC summit held in Kathmandu (Nepal)

2003: Space Shuttle Columbia of USA exploded; Kalpana Chawla of Indian origin died; Us atack on Iraq (March 19).

2004: Earthquake Tsunami Killed thousands across nine nations.

2006: Saddam Hussain is executed.

2007 : Japan launched first defence ministry since World War-II

2008: Pushpa Kamal Dahal (Prachanda) becomes the first PM of Republican Nepal 2009: Barack Obama sworn in as the 15th President of USA

2010: Dubai opened world's tallest skyscraper-Burj Khalifa; US, Russia signed nuclear arms pact.

2011: Dilma Rousseff sworn in as Brazil's first woman prez (Jan. 1); US forces killed Osama-bin-Laden in Pakistan (May 1).

2012: Myanmar pardons as number of prominent political prisoners (Jan. 13)

2013: XI Jinping takes over as China's president(March 14); Pervez Musharraf arrested in Pakistan(April 19); Nelson Mandela died (Dec.5)

2014: Sheikh Hasina is sworn in a Bangladesh PM for 3rd term(Jan.12).

2015: Pakistan House passes Army Court Bill (Jan.6); Maithripal Sirisena became new President of Sri Lanka(Jan.9); Massive earthquake hit Nepal more than 4999 dead (April 25).

THE UNIVERSE

Some Facts of the Solar System:

Number of Planets: Mercury, Venus ,Earth, Mars, Jupiter, Satum, Uranus and Neptune.

Largest most

Massive Planet- Jupiter

Brightest planet-Venus

Brightest star-Sirius

Fastest orbiting planet-Mercury

Greatest average density-Jupiter

Strongest magnetic fields-Jupiter

Most circular orbit -Venus

Shortest (synodic) day -Jupiter

Greatest amount of liquid on the surface -Earth

The Earth: Facts and Data

Composition of the Earth: Aluminium (0.4%), Sulphur (2.7%), Silicon (13%), Oxygen (28%), Calcium (1.2%), Nickel (2.7%), Magnesium (17%), Iron (35%)

Surface area : 510100500 sq km

Land Surface (29.1%) : 148950800 sq km

Ocean Surface (70.9%) : 361149700 sq km

Type of water: 97% salt, 3% fresh

Total area of water : 382672000 sq km

Equatorial diameter : 12753 km

Equatorial Circumference : 40075 km

Polar Circumference : 40007 km

Polar diameter : 12710 km

Equatorial radius : 6376 km

Polar radius : 0335 km

Mass (estimated weight) : 594×10^{19} metric tons

Mean distance from the Sun :149407000 km

Earth's orbit speed (around sun) : 107320 kmph

Period of Revolution (round the sun) : 365 days 5 hrs 48 min. 45.51 seconds

Time of rotation (on its axis) : 23 hrs 56 min 4.09 seconds

Solar Statistics

Distance from the Earth : 149.8 million km

Absolute Visual Magnitude : 4.75

Diameter Core: 1,384,000 km

Temperature Photosphere : 15000000 K

Temperature Rotation as seen from the Earth (at the equator) : 25.38 days

Rotation as seen from the Earth(near the poles) : 33 days

Chemical Composition : Hydrogen (71%) , Helium (26.5%) , Other elements (2.5%)

Age : About 4.5 billion years

Expected lifetime : About 10 billion year

Oceans of the World

Pacific : 166,241,000 sq km

Atlantic : 86,557,000 sq km

Indian : 73,427,000 sq km

Arctic : 9,485,000 sq km

Longest Rivers

Name	Country/Continent	Length in Kilometres
Nile	Africa	6690
Amazon	South America	6437
Mississippi-Missouri	USA	6020
Yangtze-Kiang	China	5494
Ob-Irtysh	Russia	5410
Hwang Ho	China	4344
Lena	Russia	4400
Niger	Africa	4180
Murray-Darling	Australia	3780
Volga	Russia	3690
St. Lawrence	Canada (USA)	4023
Orinoco	South America	2575
Danube	Europe	2850
Indus	Asia	2900

Major Riverside Cities

City	River	Country
Alexandria	Nile	Egypt
Amsterdam	Amsel	Netherland
Ankara	Kizil	Turkey
Baghdad	Tigris	Iraq
Bangkok	Menon	Thialand
Belgrade	Danube	Yugoslavia
Berlin	Spree	Germany
Budapest	Danube	Hungary
Cairo	Nile	Egypt
Chittagong	Karnaphuli	Bangladesh
Karachi	Indus	Pakistan
Khartoum	Blue & White Nile	Sudan
Lahore	Ravi	Pakistan
Lisbon	Tagus	Portugal
Liverpool	Mersey	England
London	Thamas	England
Moscow	Moskova	Russia
Orlands	Mississipi	USA
New York	Hudson	USA
Paris	Seine	France
Rangoon(Yangon)	Irawadi	Myanmar
Rome	Tiber	Italy

India's Cities, River and States

City	River	State
Agra	Yamuna	Uttar Pradesh
Ahmedabad	Sabarmati	Gujarat
Badrinath	Alkananda	Uttarakhand

Cuttack	Mahanadi	Odisha
Delhi	Yamuna	Delhi
Dibrugarh	Brahmaputra	Assam
Guwahati	Brahmaputra	Assam
Haridwar	Ganges	Uttarakhand
Hyderabad	Musi	Andhra Pradesh
Jabalpur	Narmada	Andhra Pradesh
Kanpur	Ganges	Uttar Pradesh
Kolkata	Hoogly	West Bengal
Kota	Chambal	Rajasthan
Lucknow	Gomti	Uttar Pradesh
Ludhiana	Sutlej	Punjab
Nasik	Godawari	Maharashtra
Patna	Ganga	Bihar
Sambalpur	Mahanadi	Odisha
Srinagar	Jhelum	Jammu and Kashmir
Surat	Tapti	Gujarat
Tiruchirapalli	Cauvery	Tamil Nadu
Varanasi	Ganges	Uttar Pradesh
Vijayawada	Krishna	Andhra Pradesh

Largest Deserts of the World

Subtropical		
Name	**Country/Continent**	**Area**
Sahara	North Africa	94,00,000 sq. km.
Kalahari	Southern Africa	9,00,000 sq. km.
Thar	India/Pakistan	2,00,000 sq. km.
Great Sandy	Australia	4,00,000 sq. km.
Cool Coastal		
Atacama,	Chile/South Africa	1,40,000 sq. km.
Cool Winter		
Gobi	China	13,00,000 sq.

			km.
Colorado (Painted Desert)		Western USA	3,37,000 sq. km.

Atmosphere

Composition of Gases in Atmosphere

Name	Composition
Nitrogen	78.03%
Oxygen	20.99%
Argon	0.93%
Carbon Dioxide	0.03%
Hydrogen	0.01%
Neon	0.0018%
Helium	0.0005%
Crypton	0.0001%
Xenon	0.000,005%
Ozone	0.000,0001%

Principal Mountain Peaks of the World

Mountains	Height in Metres	Range	Date of First Ascent
Mount Everest	8,848	Himalayas	May 29, 1953
K-2(Godwin Austen)	8,611	Karakoram	July 31, 1954
Kanchenjunga	8,597	Himalayas	May 25, 1955
Lhotse	8,511	Himalayas	May 18, 1956
Makalu-I	8,481	Himalayas	May 15,1955
Dhaulagiri-I	8,167	Himalayas	May 13, 1960
Mansalu-I	8,156	Himalayas	May 9, 1956
Chollyo	8,153	Himalayas	October 19, 1954

Nanga Parbat	8,124	Himalayas	July 3, 1953
Annapurna-I	8,091	Himalayas	July 3, 1950
Gasherbhum-I	8,068	Karakoram	July 5, 1958
Broad Peak-I	8,047	Karakoram	July 9, 1957
Gasherbhum-II	8,034	Karakoram	July 7, 1956
Shisha Pangma (Gosainthan)	8,014	Himalayas	May 2, 1964
Gasherbhum-III	7,952	Karakoram	August 11, 1975

International Date Line

It generally relates to 180°E or W meridian of longitude which falls on the contrary side of the Greenwich meridian and the date changes by one day (for example 24 hours), as this line is crossed. On crossing this line from east to west a day is added, and a day is subtracted on crossing it from west to east.

Important Boundary Lines

Boundary Line	Countries
Durand Line	Pakistan and Afghanistan
Hindenberg Line	Germany and Poland
Maginot Line	France and Germany
Mannerhein Line	Russia and Finland
Mc Mahon Line	India and China
Order Niesse Line	Germany and Poland
Radcliff Line	India and Pakistan
Seigfrid Line	Germany and France
17th Parallel	North Vietnam and South Vietnam (Before United)
38th Parallel	North Korea and South Korea
49th Parallel	USA and Canada

Famous Straits of the World

Strait	Between	Country
Malacca	Andaman Sea and South China Sea	Indonesia
Magellan Strait	Pacific and South Atlantic Ocean	Chile
Palk Strait	Mannar and Bay of Bengal	India and Sri Lanka
Dover Strait	English Channel and North Sea	England and France
Berring Strait	Berring Sea and Chukasi Sea	Alaska and Russia
Sugaroo Strait	Japan Sea and Pacific Ocean	Japan
Sunda Strait	Java and Indian Ocean	Indonesia
Gibralter Strait	Mediterranean Sea and Atlantic Ocean	Spain
Harmuj Strait	Persia and Bay of Oman	Oman and Iran
Hudson Strait	Bay of Hudson and Atlantic Ocean	Canada

World's Famous Official Documents

White Paper: India; Orange Book: Netherlands; Yellow Book: France **Green Book: Italy and Iran; White Book:** Portugal, China and Germany **Grey Book:** Japan and Belgium.

Famous Newspapers of the World

Newspaper	Place of Publishing	Language
Al-Ahram	Cairo (Egypt)	Arabic
Daily News	New York (USA)	English
Daily Mirror	Britain	English
Guardian	London(Britain)	English
Merdeca	Jakarta(Indonesia)	Indonesian
New Statesman	Britain	English
Pravada	Moscow(Russia)	Russian

People's Daily	Beijing(China)	Chinese
Hindu, Times of India, Tribune, Statesman, Indian Express, Economic Times Hindustan, Nav Bharat Times, Rashtriya Sahara, Dainik Jagaran,	India	English
Punjab Kesari	India	Hindi

National Emblems of Important Countries

Country	National Emblem
America	Golden Rod
Australia	Kangaroo
Ireland	Shamrock
Italy	White Lily
Isreal	Candelabrum
Iran	Rose
Canada	White Lily
Great Britain	Rose
Chile	Candor and Huemul
Germany	Corn Flower
Japan	Chrysanthemum
Zimbabwe	Zimbabwe Bird
Denmark	Beach
Turkey	Crescent and Star
Netherlands	Lion
New Zealand	Kiwi
Norway	Lion
Nepal	Kurti
Pakistan	Crescent
Polond	Eagle
France	Lily
Belgium	Lion
Bangladesh	Water Lily
Mongolia	The Soyombo
Russia	Double Headed Eagle
India	Lioned Capital

Syria	Eagle

Continent of the World

Name	Area(Sq. km)
Asia	44,485,900
Africa	30,259,680
Europe	10,530,750
North America	24,235,280
South America	17,820,770
Australia	7,830,682
Antarctica	14,000,000

INDIAN CONSTITUTION AND POLITY

The Indian Constitution is a comprehensive document and it is the lengthiest composed Constitution in the World.

The Preamble of the Constitution: We the people of India, having solemnly resolved to Constitute India into a Sovereign, Socialist, Secular Democratic Republic and to secure to all its citizens: **Justice:** Social, economic and political; **Liberty:** Thought, expression, belief, faith and worship; **Equality:** Status and opportunity, and promote among them all; **Fraternity:** Assuring the dignity of the individual and the unity and integrity of the nation. In our Constituent Assembly, this twenty-sixth day of November, 1949, do hereby adopt, enact and give to ourselves this constitution.

Parliament: Parliament is the national legislature of the Indian Union. It consists of two Houses known as the Council of States or the Rajya Sabha and the House of People or Lok Sabha.

Rajya Sabha: Rajya Sabha is the Upper House of the Parliament and it is comprised of representatives from the States or the Constituent units of the Indian Union. It is a permanent body, 33% of 'its members resigning after every two years. Its most extreme quality is 250. Out of these, twelve members are nominated by the President from notable personalities in the domain of Science, Art, Literature and Social Service. Rest of 238 representatives of the States and Union' Territories are elected.

Lok Sabha: The Lok Sabha whose life is five years, is the Lower House of Parliament and includes individuals straightforwardly elected by the people. The House of the people (Lok Sabha) at present comprises of 545 members from these, 530 members are straightforwardly elected from the states and 13 from Union Territories while 2 are nominated by the President from Anglo-Indian community. The House of the People shall continue for five years (unless sooner dissolved) from the date of meeting and no longer and the expiry the said period of 5 years shall operate as dissolution of the House.

Parliamentary Committees:

There are a few Parliamentary Committees to help the Parliament its thoughts. These are appointed, elected by the respective Houses of Lok Sabha and Rajya Sabha on a motion made or are nominated by their presiding officers, i.e., the Speaker Lok Sabha and the Chairman of Rajya Sabha individually. Extensively, Parliamentary Committees are of sorts standing panels and specially appointed advisory groups.Parliamentary Committees are of kinds standing committees and ad-hoc committees. Among the, Standing Committees, there are financial Committees: (i) Public Account Committee; (ii) Estimate Committee; (iii) Public undertaking Committee. Ad-hoc Committees are appointment the need emerges and stop to exist the work is finished.

President

The president is the Constitutional head of the Republic of India. Really speaking, he is the constitutional head, but not the real executive.The real power is vested in the hands of the Council of Ministers.

Qualifications: (i) Indian citizen, (ii) age not less than 35 years, (iii) should have qualified for election to the Lok Sabha, (iv) should not hold any office of profit, (v) should not be a Member of Parliament or State Legislature.

Powers: He makes appointments to all the constitutional posts. He can address either House of Parliament and dissolve Lok Sabha. All Bills passed by Parliament must receive his assent to become an Act. He issues ordinances when Parliament is not in session. He President holds the office for a period of 5 years. He is eligible for re-election. He can declare national emergency, state emergency and financial emergency. He can pardon death.

List of Presidents of India

No.	Name (birth–death)	Took office	Left office	Time (in office)	Party	Subject related to President
1.	Rajendra	26	13 May	12 years,	Indian	Prasad, from Bihar, was the first

	Prasad (1884–1963)	January 1950	1962	107 days	National Congress	president of independent India and also the longest-serving president, as the only president to serve two or more terms in office.He was also a freedom fighter during the Indian independence movement.
2.	Sarvepalli Radhakrishnan (1888–1975)	13 May 1962	13 May 1967	5 years	Independent	Radhakrishnan was a prominent philosopher and writer and also held the position of vice-chancellor of the Andhra University and Banaras Hindu University. He received the Bharat Ratna award in 1954 before becoming the President.He was the first president from South India.
3.	Zakir Husain (1897–1969)	13 May 1967	3 May 1969	1 year, 355 days	Independent	Husain was vice-chancellor of the Aligarh Muslim University and a recipient of Padma Vibhushan and Bharat Ratna.He died in office, the first to do so. He was also the shortest-serving President. He was also the first Muslim President.
4.	Varahagiri	3 May	20 July	78	–	He was elected Vice President of

	Venkata Giri (1894–1980)	1969	1969	days		India in 1967. Following the death of President Zakir Husain, Giri was appointed as Acting President. He resigned after a few months to take part in the presidential elections
5.	Mohammad Hidayatullah (1905–1992)	20 July 1969	24 August 1969	35 days	–	Hidayatullah served as the Chief Justice of India and was also a recipient of the Order of the British Empire.He served as Acting President until the election of Giri as the President of India.
6.	Varahagiri Venkata Giri (1894–1980)	24 August 1969	24 August 1974	5 years	–	Giri was the first person to have served as both an acting president and president of India. He was a recipient of the Bharat Ratna, and served as Labour and Employment Minister and High Commissioner to Ceylon (Sri Lanka).
7.	Fakhruddin Ali Ahmed (1905–1977)	24 August 1974	11 February 1977	2 years 171 days	Indian National Congress	Ahmed served as a Minister before being elected as president. He died in 1977 before his term of office ended, and was the second Indian president to die in office.He was also president during

						Emergency
8.	Basappa Danappa Jatti (1912–2002)	11 February 1977	25 July 1977	164 days	–	Jatti was the vice president of India during Ahmed's term of office, and was sworn in as Acting President upon Ahmed's death. He earlier served as the Chief Minister for the State of Mysore State.
9.	Neelam Sanjiva Reddy (1913–1996)	25 July 1977	25 July 1982	5 years	Janata Party	Reddy was the first Chief Minister of Andhra Pradesh. Reddy was the only Member of Parliament from the Janata Party to get elected from Andhra Pradesh. He was unanimously elected Speaker of the Lok Sabha on 26 March 1977 and relinquished this office on 13 July 1977 to become the 6th President of India
10.	Zail Singh (1916–1994)	25 July 1982	25 July 1987	5 years	Indian National Congress	In March 1972, Singh assumed the position of Chief Minister of Punjab, and in 1980, he became Union Home Minister. He was also secretary general to Non-Aligned Movement (NAM) from 1983 to 1986.

11.	Ramaswamy Venkataraman (1910–2009)	25 July 1987	25 July 1992	5 years	Indian National Congress	In 1942, Venkataraman was jailed by the British for his involvement in the Indian independence movement. After his release, he was elected to independent India's Provisional Parliament as a member of the Congress Party in 1950 and eventually joined the central government, where he first served as Minister of Finance and Industry and later as Minister of Defence.
12.	Shankar Dayal Sharma (1918–1999)	25 July 1992	25 July 1997	5 years	Indian National Congress	Sharma was Chief Minister of Madhya Pradesh, and the Indian Minister for Communications. He also served as the Governor of Andhra Pradesh, Punjab and Maharashtra
13.	Kocheril Raman Narayanan (1921–2005)	25 July 1997	25 July 2002	5 years	Independent	Narayanan served as India's ambassador to Thailand, Turkey, China and United States of America. He received doctorates in Science and Law and was also a chancellor in several universities.

						He was also the vice-chancellor of Jawaharlal Nehru University. He was the first Dalit President
14.	Avul Pakir Jainulabdeen Abdul Kalam (1931–2015)	25 July 2002	25 July 2007	5 years	Independent	Kalam was an educator and engineer who played a leading role in the development of India's ballistic missile and nuclear weapons programs. He also received the Bharat Ratna. He was popularly known as"People's President
15.	Pratibha Patil (1934–)	25 July 2007	25 July 2012	5 years	Indian National Congress	Patil was the first woman to become the President of India. She was also the first female governor of Rajasthan.
16.	Pranab Mukherjee (1935–2020)	25 July 2012	25 July 2017	5 years	Indian National Congress	Mukherjee held various posts in the cabinet ministry for the Government of India such as Finance Minister, Foreign Minister, Defence Minister and Deputy Chairman of the Planning Commission.
17.	Ram Nath Kovind (1945–)	25 July 2017	25 July 2022)	5 years	Bharatiya Janata Party	Kovind was governor of Bihar from 2015 to 2017 and a Member of Parliament from 1994 to 2006. He is

						the second Dalit president (after K. R. Narayanan) and is the first president from the Bharatiya Janata Party.
18.	Smt. Droupadi Murmu (1958--	25 July 2022	Incumbent *To be ended on 25 July 2027)*	-	Bharatiya Janata Party	Droupadi Murmu is an Indian politician who is serving as the 15th and current President of India since 25 July 2022. She is a member of the Bharatiya Janata Party. She is the first person belonging to the tribal community and also the second woman after Pratibha Patil to hold the office.

Vice-president

The Vice-President as the ex-officio of India, Chairman of the Council of States and should be eligible for election as a (Rajya Sabha). He is elected by an electoral consisting of the of the member of both Houses of Parliament in accordance with the system of proportional representation by means of the single transferable vote. He must be a citizen Supreme Court not less than 35 years of age, and should be eligible for the election of a president or a vice-president are to be a dealt with in accordance with Article-71.

List of Vice Presidents of India

No.	Name (birth-death)	Took office	Left office	Term (in years)	President(s)	Party
1.	Sarvepalli Radhakrishnan	13 May 1952	12 May 1957	10	Rajendra Prasad	Independent

	(1888–1975)					
2.	Zakir Husain (1897–1969)	13 May 1962	12 May 1967	5	Sarvepalli Radhakrishnan	Independent
3.	V. V. Giri (1894–1980)	13 May 1967	3 May 1969	2	Zakir Husain	Independent
4.	V. V. Giri (1894–1980)	13 May 1967	3 May 1969	2	Zakir Husain	Independent
5.	B. D. Jatti (1912–2002)	31 August 1974	30 August 1979	5	Fakhruddin Ali Ahmed (1974-1977) Neelam Sanjiva Reddy (1977-1979)	Indian National Congress
6.	Mohammad Hidayatullah (1905–1992)	31 August 1979	30 August 1984	5	Neelam Sanjiva Reddy (1979-1982) Zail Singh (1982-1984)	Independent
7.	R. Venkataraman (1910–2009)	31 August 1984	24 July 1987	3	Zail Singh	Indian National Congress
8.	Shankar Dayal Sharma (1918–1999)	3 September 1987	24 July 1992	5	R.Venkataraman	Indian National Congress
9.	K. R. Narayanan(1921–2005)	21 August 1992	24 July 1997	5	Shankar Dayal Sharma	Indian National Congress
10.	Krishan Kant (1927–2002)	21 August 1997	27 July 2002	5	K. R. Narayanan (1997–2002) Avul Pakir Jainulabdeen Abdul Kalam (2002)	Janata Dal
11.	Bhairon Singh Shekhawat (1924–2010)	19 August 2002	21 July 2007	5	Avul Pakir Jainulabdeen Abdul Kalam	Bharatiya Janata Party
12.	Mohammad Hamid Ansari (1937–)	11 August 2007	11 August 2017	10	Pratibha Patil (2007–2012) Pranab Mukherjee (2012–2017) Ram Nath Kovind (2017)	Indian National Congress
13.	Venkaiah Naidu	11 August 2017	10 August 2022	5	Ram Nath Kovind	Bharatiya Janata Party

	(1949–)					
14.	Jagdeep Dhankhar	11 August 2022	Incumbent	-	Smt. Droupadi Murmu	Bharatiya Janata Party

Prime Minister

The Constitution lays down that there shall be a Council of Ministers Headed by Prime Minister to aid and advise the President in the exercise of his functions. The Prime Minister is the head of the Cabinet.Other Ministers are appointed by the President on his advise. He is the leader of the majority party in the Lok Sabha.

Name (Birth–Death) Constituency	Party (Alliance)	Term of office			Appointed by
Jawaharlal Nehru (1889–1964) Phulpur, Uttar Pradesh	Indian National Congress	15 August 1947	15 April 1952	16 years, 286 days	Lord Mountbatten
		15 April 1952	17 April 1957	ys	Rajendra Prasad
		17 April 1957	2 April 1962		
		2 April 1962	27 May 1964		
Gulzarilal Nanda (acting) (1898–1998) Sabarkantha, Gujarat	Indian National Congress	27 May 1964	9 June 1964	13 days	Sarvepalli Radhakrishnan
Lal Bahadur Shastri (1904–1966) Allahabad, Uttar Pradesh	Indian National Congress	9 June 1964	11 January 1966	1 year, 216 days	
Gulzarilal Nanda (acting)	Indian National	11 January	24 January	13 days	

(1898–1998) Sabarkantha, Gujarat	Congress	1966	1966		
Indira Gandhi (1917–1984) Rajya Sabha MP for Uttar Pradesh (1966-67) Rae Bareli, Uttar Pradesh	Indian National Congress/Indian National Congress (R)	24 January 1966	4 March 1967	11 years, 59 days	
		4 March 1967	15 March 1971		
		15 March 1971	24 March 1977		V. V. Giri
Morarji Desai (1896–1995) Surat, Gujarat	Janata Party	24 March 1977	28 July 1979	2 years, 126 days	B. D. Jatti (acting)
Charan Singh (1902–1987) Baghpat, Uttar Pradesh	Janata Party (Secular) with INC (I)	28 July 1979	14 January 1980	170 days	Neelam Sanjiva Reddy
Indira Gandhi (1917–1984) Medak, Andhra Pradesh (now Telangana)	Indian National Congress (I)	14 January 1980	31 October 1984	4 years, 291 days	
Rajiv Gandhi (1944–1991) Amethi, Uttar Pradesh	Indian National Congress (I)	31 October 1984	31 December 1984	5 years, 32 days	Zail Singh
		31 December 1984	2 December 1989		
Vishwanath Pratap Singh (1931–2008) Fatehpur, Uttar Pradesh	Janata Dal (National Front)	2 December 1989	10 November 1990	343 days	Ramaswamy Venkataraman
Chandra Shekhar	Samajwadi	10	21 June	223	

(1927–2007) Ballia, Uttar Pradesh	Janata Party (Rashtriya) with INC (I)	November 1990	1991	days	
P. V. Narasimha Rao (1921–2004) Nandyal, Andhra Pradesh	Indian National Congress (I)	21 June 1991	16 May 1996	4 years, 330 days	
Atal Bihari Vajpayee (1924–2018) Lucknow, Uttar Pradesh	Bharatiya Janata Party	16 May 1996	1 June 1996	16 days	Shankar Dayal Sharma
H. D. Deve Gowda (1933–) Rajya Sabha MP for Karnataka	Janata Dal (United Front)	1 June 1996	21 April 1997	324 days	
Inder Kumar Gujral (1919–2012) Rajya Sabha MP for Bihar	Janata Dal (United Front)	21 April 1997	19 March 1998	332 days	
Atal Bihari Vajpayee (1924–2018) Lucknow, Uttar Pradesh	Bharatiya Janata Party (NDA)	19 March 1998	10 October 1999	6 years, 64 days	K. R. Narayanan
		10 October 1999	22 May 2004		
Manmohan Singh (1932–) Rajya Sabha MP for Assam	Indian National Congress (UPA)	22 May 2004	22 May 2009	10 years, 4 days	A. P. J. Abdul Kalam
		22 May 2009	26 May 2014		Pratibha Patil
Narendra Modi (1950–) Varanasi, Uttar	Bharatiya Janata Party (NDA)	26 May 2014	30 May 2019	6 years, 28 day	Pranab Mukherjee
		30 May	Incumb		Ram Nath

Pradesh		2019	ent	s	Kovind
					Smt.
					Droupadi
					Murmu

Attorney General of India: The Attorney General of India will be law official of the Government of India. In spite of he is not a member of the cabinet, he has the option to talk in the House of Parliament, however he has no privilege to cast a vote. The Attorney General of India shall be appointed by the President and shall hold office during his pleasure. His duty shall be to give advice on such legal matter from time to time as may be referred to him by the President.

The Comptroller and Auditor General of India: The Comptroller and Auditor General of India is the watchman of the the public purse and it is his obligation to see that not a paisa is spent out of the the consolidated fund of India or of a state without the authority appropriate legislature. He is appointed by the President of India.

Speaker of Lok Sabha: Speaker is chosen by the Lok Sabha from among its members. The Speaker will have the final power to maintain order within the House of the People and to interpret its rules of procedure. Speaker decides whether a bill is a money bill or a non money bill.

The Governor: The Governor is appointed by the President and holds office during the pleasure of the President. Aside from the power to appoint the council of ministers, if the governor finds that the government of state cannot be carried on in accordance with the provisions of the constitution (Art. 356), he may send his report to the President who may assume to himself the functions of the government of the state.

Inter-state Councils: Article 263 provides for inter-state councils. The power of the President to set up Inter-State Councils not only for advising upon disputes but also for investigating and discussing subjects in which some or all of the states, or the Union and one or more of the states have common interest.

Schedules to the Constitution:

The Constitution of India originally contained only eight schedules. Presently there are 12 schedules in the constitution.

First Schedule: This Schedule is related to the States and Union territories.

Second Schedule: This Schedule is related to salary and allowances of the President, Governors, Speaker, Supreme Court and High Court Judges etc.

Third Schedule: This Schedule contains forms of oath and affirmation.

Fourth Schedule: This Schedule contains allocation of seats to each State and Union territory in the Council of States.

Fifth Schedule: This Schedule is related for administration and control of Scheduled areas and scheduled tribes.

Sixth Schedule: This Schedule is related for administration of Tribal Areas in Assam, Meghalaya and Mizoram.

Seventh Schedule: This Schedule is related for Distribution of powers and functions between the Centre and state governments under three lists.

Eight Schedule: This Schedule is related to the languages recognized by Parliament.

Ninth Schedule: It contains laws passed by the Union or States which cannot be taken to the courts.

Tenth Schedule: This Schedule is related to the provisions as to disqualification on the ground of political defection.

Eleventh Schedule: This Schedule is related to the provisions regarding powers, authority, etc. of Panchayati Raj institutions.

Twelfth Schedule: This Schedule is related to the provisions regarding powers, authority, etc. of Municipalities etc.

Fundamental Rights:

1. Right to Equality: No special privileges, no distinction on grounds of religion, caste, creed and sex.

2.Right to Freedom: The right to freedom of expression and speech, the right to choose one's own profession, the right to reside in any part of the Indian Union.

3.Right to Freedom to Religion: Except when it is in the interest of public order, morality, health or other conditions, everybody has the right to profess, practice and propagate his religion freely.

4.Cultural and Educational Rights: The Constitution provides that every community can run its own institutions to preserve its own culture and language.

5.Right against Exploitation: Traffic in human beings and forced labour and the employment of children under 14 years in factories or mines, are punishable offences.

6. Rights to Constitutional Remedies: When a citizen finds that any of his fundamental rights has been encroached upon, he can move the Supreme Court, which has been empowered to safeguard the fundamental rights of a citizen (Article 32).

Fundamental Duties:

Fundamental duties for the Indian been incorporated in the through the Constitution Amendment Act, 1976. These duties are: (i) abiding by the Constitution and respect its ideals and institutions, the National Flag and the National Anthem; (ii) cherishing and following the noble deeds which inspired our national strrugle for freedom ; (iii) upholding the sovereignty, unity and integrity of India; (iv) defending the country and render national service when called upon to do so; (v) promoting harmony and the spirit of common brotherhood amongst all the transcending religious, regional diversities and to renounce practices derogatory to the dignity of women; (vi) riching heritage of our composite (vii) protecting and improving natural environment including forests, and wildlife, and to have for living creatures; (viii) developing the scientific temper, humanism and the spirit of inquiry and reform; (ix) safeguaring public property and to abjure violence; (x) striving towards excellence in all spheres of individual and collective activity so that the nation constantly rises to higher levels of endeavour and achievement; (xi) providing oppertunity for education to his child or,as the case may be, ward between age of six and fourteen years

Directive Principles of State Policy

The Directive Principles of State Policy are contained in Article 36 to 51 in Part IV of the constitution. Directive principles are not enforceable through courts. Main aim of Directive Principles is to provide social welfare for our society.

Some Important facts regarding Directive Principles:

- ➤ Provisions for adequate means of livelihood for all citizens (Art.39)
- ➤ Right to work (Art.41)
- ➤ Right to human condition of work and maternity relief(Art.42)
- ➤ Right to a living wage and condition of work ensuring decent standard of life of worker (Art. 43)
- ➤ Common Civil Code (Art. 44)
- ➤ Prohibit consumption of liquor (Art. 47)
- ➤ Prevent slaughter of useful cattle (Art. 48)
- ➤ Organise Panchayati Raj (Art. 40)
- ➤ Separate the judiciary from the executive (Art. 50)
- ➤ Protect and maintain places of historic monuments (Art.51)
- ➤ International peace (Art. 51)

Union Public Service Commission (U.P.S.C.)

The Commission is answerable for i) recruitment to all civil services and posts, under the Union Government by examina(tions, interviews and promotions, and (ii) advising the Government on all matters methods of recruitnent, principles followed in making promotions and transfers. Its Chairman is appointed by the President.

Staff Selection Commission

The Union Government has established the Staff Selection Commission for enlistment to non-specialized Group C and some of Group B posts in the central departments and in subordinate workplaces. The administrative Reforms Commission had suggested the setting up of such a Commission.

Supreme Court of India

1. Supreme Court of India, the highest Court of India, consists of a Chief Justice and not more than 30 Judges appointed by the President.

2. The Judges hold office till the age of 65.

3. For the appointment as a Judge of the Supreme Court, a person must be a citizen of India and must have been for at least five years a Judge of a High Court or Advocate of a High Court for at least ten years or he must be, in the opinion ^{the} president, a distinguished jurist.

No	Name (birth–death)	Period of office		Length of term (days)	Appointed by (President of India)
1	H. J. Kania (1890–1951)	26 January 1950	6 November 1951	649	Rajendra Prasad
2	M. Patanjali Sastri (1889–1963)	7 November 1951	3 January 1954	788	
3	Mehr Chand Mahajan (1889–1967)	4 January 1954	22 December 1954	352	
4	Bijan Kumar Mukherjea (1891–1956)	23 December 1954	31 January 1956	404	
5	Sudhi Ranjan Das (1894–1977)	1 February 1956	30 September 1959	1337	
6	Bhuvaneshwar Prasad Sinha (1899–1986)	1 October 1959	31 January 1964	1583	
7	P. B. Gajendragadkar (1901–1981)	1 February 1964	15 March 1966	773	Sarvepalli Radhakrishnan
8	Amal Kumar Sarkar (1901–2001)	16 March 1966	29 June 1966	105	
9	Koka Subba Rao (1902–1976)	30 June 1966	11 April 1967	285	
10	Kailas Nath Wanchoo	12 April	24 February	318	

	(1903–1988)	1967	1968		
11	Mohammad Hidayatullah (1905–1992)[2]	25 February 1968	16 December 1970	1025	Zakir Hussain
12	Jayantilal Chhotalal Shah (1906–1991)	17 December 1970	21 January 1971	35	Varahagiri Venkata Giri
13	Sarv Mittra Sikri (1908–1992)	22 January 1971	25 April 1973	824	
14	A. N. Ray (1912–2009)	26 April 1973	27 January 1977	1372	
15	Mirza Hameedullah Beg (1913–1988)	29 January 1977	21 February 1978	389	Fakhruddin Ali Ahmed
16	Y. V. Chandrachud (1920–2008)	22 February 1978	11 July 1985	2696	Neelam Sanjiva Reddy
17	P. N. Bhagwati (1921–2017)	12 July 1985	20 December 1986	526	Zail Singh
18	Raghunandan Swarup Pathak (1924–2007)	21 December 1986	18 June 1989‡	940	
19	Engalaguppe Seetharamiah Venkataramiah (1924–1997)	19 June 1989	17 December 1989	181	Ramaswamy Venkataraman
20	Sabyasachi Mukharji (1927–1990)	18 December 1989	25 September 1990	281	
21	Ranganath Misra (1926–2012)	26 September 1990	24 November 1991	424	
22	Kamal Narain Singh (1926–)	25 November 1991	12 December 1991	17	
23	Madhukar Hiralal Kania (1927–2016)	13 December 1991	17 November 1992	340	

24	Lalit Mohan Sharma (1928–2008)	18 November 1992	11 February 1993	85	Shankar Dayal Sharma
25	M. N. Venkatachaliah (1929–)	12 February 1993	24 October 1994	619	
26	Aziz Mushabber Ahmadi (1932–)	25 October 1994	24 March 1997	881	
27	J. S. Verma (1933–2013)	25 March 1997	17 January 1998	298	
28	Madan Mohan Punchhi (1933–2015)	18 January 1998	9 October 1998	264	Kocheril Raman Narayanan
29	Adarsh Sein Anand (1936–2017)	10 October 1998	31 October 2001	1,117	
30	Sam Piroj Bharucha (1937–)	1 November 2001	5 May 2002	185	
31	Bhupinder Nath Kirpal (1937–)	6 May 2002	7 November 2002	185	
32	Gopal Ballav Pattanaik (1937–)	8 November 2002	18 December 2002	40	A. P. J. Abdul Kalam
33	V. N. Khare (1939–)	19 December 2002	1 May 2004	499	
34	S. Rajendra Babu (1939–)	2 May 2004	31 May 2004	29	
35	Ramesh Chandra Lahoti (1940–)	1 June 2004	31 October 2005	517	
36	Yogesh Kumar Sabharwal (1942–2015)	1 November 2005	13 January 2007	438	
37	K. G. Balakrishnan (1945–)	14 January 2007	12 May 2010	1,214	
38	S. H. Kapadia (1947–2016)	12 May 2010	28 September 2012	870	Pratibha Patil
39	Altamas Kabir	29 September	18 July 2013	292	Pranab

	(1948–2017)	2012			Mukherjee
40	P. Sathasivam (1949–)	19 July 2013	26 April 2014	281	
41	Rajendra Mal Lodha (1949–)	27 April 2014	27 September 2014	153	
42	H. L. Dattu (1950–)	28 September 2014	2 December 2015	430	
43	T. S. Thakur (1952–)	3 December 2015	3 January 2017	397	
44	Jagdish Singh Khehar (1952–)	4 January 2017	27 August 2017	235	
45	Dipak Misra (1953–)	28 August 2017	2 October 2018	400	Ram Nath Kovind
46	Ranjan Gogoi (1954–)	3 October 2018	17 November 2019	410	
47	Sharad Arvind Bobde (1956–)	18 November 2019	23 April 2021	521	
48	Nuthalapati Venkata Ramana (1957–)	24 April 2021	26 August 2022	489	
49	Uday Umesh Lalit (1957–)	27 August 2022	Incumbent	-	Smt.Droupadi Murmu

DEFENCE

The Supreme Command of the Armed vested in the possession of the President of the Country. The responsibility for national defence, however, rests with the Cabinet. Extremely significant inquiries having a direction on guard are chosen by Cabinet Committee on Political, which is presided over by the Prime Minister.The Defense Minister is dependable to Parliament for all issues concerning the Defense Services. All the administrative and operational control of Armed Forces are practiced by the Ministry of Defense. The three services-Army, Navy and Air Force function through their respective service headquarters headed by the chief headquarters headed by the chief.

Commissioned Ranks in Defence Services

Army	Navy	Air Force
General	Admiral	Air Chief Marshal
Lieutenant-General	Vice-Admiral	Air Marshal
Major-General	Rear-Admiral	Air Vice-Marshal
Brigadier	Commodor	Air Commodor
Colonel	Captain	Group Captain
Lieutenant-Colonel	Commander	Wing Commander
Major	Lt.Commander	Squadron Leader
Captain	Lieutenant	Flight Lieutenant
Lieutenant	Sub-Lieutenant	Flying Officer

Internal Security Organisations of India

Sl. No.	Name of Organisation	Year of Creation	Headquarters
1.	Assam Rifles (A.R)	1835	Shillong
2.	Central Reserve Police Force (C.R.P.F.)	1939	New Delhi
3.	Territorial Army	1948	In different States
4.	Indo-Tibetan Border Police	1962	New Delhi
5.	Home Guard	1962	In different States
6.	Coast Guard	1978	New Delhi

7.	Border Security Force (B.S.F.)	1965	New Delhi
8.	Central Industrial Security Force (C.I.S.F.)	1969	New Delhi
9.	National Security Guard	1984	New Delhi

Commander-in-Chiefs of India
1. General Roy Bucher   Jan. 1, 1948 - Jan. 14, 1949
2. General K.M. Kariappa   Jan.15-1949 - Jan.14,1953
3. General Maharaj Rajendra Sinhji   Jan. 15, 1953 - March 31,1955
4. First Marshal of the Indian Air Force   Arjan Singh

First Chiefs of Staff of Indian Forces
1. General Maharaj Rajendra Sinhji (Army Staff)   April1,1955 - May14,1955
2.Vice Admiral R D. Katari (Naval Staff)   April 22, 1958- June 4, 1962
3. Air Marshal Sri.Thomas Elmherst (Air Staff)   Aug.15,1947 - Feb. 21, 1950

Army Institutes

Rashffiya Indian -Milinry College (prepare for enfrance to N.D.A)	Dehradun
National Defence Academy (three services)	Khadakwasla,Pune
Indian Military Academy (Army)	Dehradun
Officers Training Academy (3 services) Short Courses	Chennai
National Defence College	New Delhi
The College of Combat	Mhow
The College of Military Engineering	Kirkee
Military College of Telecommunication Engineering	Mhow
The armoured Corps Centre and School	Ahmed Nagar

The School Artillery	Deolali
The Infantry School	Mhow and Belgaum
College of Material Management	Jabalpur

Air Force Institutions

Air Force Academy	Hyderabad
HelicopterTraining School	Hakimpet
Flying Instructors School	Tambaram, Chenni
The College of Air Warfare	Secunderabad
Air Force Administrative College	Coimbatore
Air Force Technical College	Jalahalli

Defence Production Units

Name	Place
Bharat Dynamites Ltd.	Hyderabad
Praga Tools	Hyderabad
Mishra Dattu Nigam	Hyderabad
Bharat Electronics Ltd.	Bangalore
Bharath Earthmovers Ltd	Bangalore
Heavy Vehicles Ltd.	Avadi, Chenni
Garden Reach Ship Builders and Engineers Ltd.	Kolkata
Mazagaon Dock	Mumbai
Goa Shipyard	Marmugao
Hindustan Shipyard Ltd.	Vishakhapatnam
Hindustan Aeronautics Ltd.	Bangalore, Hyderabad, Nasik, Koraput, Kanpur, Lucknow

Special Status of Some Indian States State

State	Year of Receiving the Special Status	State	Year of Receiving the Special Status
Assam	1969	Tripura	1972
Nagaland	1969	Sikkim	1975-76
Jammu& Kashmir	1969	Mizoram	1986-87
Himachal Pradesh	1971	Arunachal Pradesh	1986-87
Manipur	1972	Uttarakhand	2001-02
Meghalaya	1972		

TRANSPORT

Important Facts of Railways:

1.Indian Railways are the biggest national undertaking.

2. The first Indian railway train rolled on its 34 km track from Mumbai to Thane on April 16, 1853.

3. Indian Railway System is largest railway system in Asia and second in the world (first America).

4. The Chittaranjan Locomotive works, first of its sort in the nation, was set up after autonomy on January 26,1950 yet now electric motors are made here.First of all it produced steam motors.

5. The number of stations, at present, is the 95% of the traveler populace, is 7,146.

6. The total length of Indian railways is 64,600 km.

7. Railway finance is separate since 1924-25 from the general revenue.

8. The only oldest running engine is Fairy Queen.

9. The first electric train rolled on from Mumbai to Kurla on 3rd February, 1925.

10. Kolkata Metro Rail is the first under ground rail.

11. Delhi Metro Railways started on 24th December, 2002.

12. The longest railway platform of the world is Gorakhpur. Its length 1355.4 m.

13. The longest tunnel of Indian railway on Konkan Railways is 6.5 km long.

14. Indian Railway Board was established in 1905.

15. Indian Railways have three gauges - Broad gauge, metre gauge and narrow gauge.

16. In railways, there are A.C., first class and second class. Third class was removed in 1974.

Zones and Headquarters of Indian Railways

1. Central : Mumbai (Victoria Terminus)

2. Eastern : Kolkata

3. Northern : New Delhi

4. North-Eastern : Gorakhpur

5. North-East Frontier : Maligaon, Guwahati

6. Southern : Chennai

7. South-Central : Secunderabad

8. South-Eastern : Kolkata

9. Western : Mumbai, Churchgate

10. East Coast : Bhubaneswar

11. East Central : Hajipur

12. North Central : Allahabad

13. North Western : Jaipur

14. South Western : Bangaluru (Hubli)

15. West Central: Jabalpur

16. South East Central : Bilaspur

17. Metro Railway: Kolkata

Important Facts of Road Transport:

1. The road network in India is one of the largest in the world.
2. The total length of roads, at present is 46.90 lakh km.
3. The Border Roads Organization (BRO) is a road construction executive force.
4. The Central Government owns the responsibility of 79,116 km long national
highways.
5. Border Road Organisation was established in 1960.

6. In spite of the fact that the national interstates don't establish even 2 percent of the all out street length of the nation, they bear about 40% of the traffic.

7. In our nation, Maharashtra has the most noteworthy length of streets (3,61,893 km) while the least length of street has Lakshadweep (1 km.).

8. National Highways Development Project has been propelled to interface the four corners of the nation by four or six paths in a system. The four significant urban communities - Kolkata, Delhi, Chennai and Mumbai will be connected by 5,882 km long streets in brilliant quadrilateral.

9. Indian streets have been isolated into three sections (a) National Highways (b)

Public Highways (c) Border Roads.

10. The all out length of streets in Delhi is 26,582 km.

Important Facts of Shipping :

1. India has 7,516 km long coast line.

2. Shipping Corporation of India is the biggest shipping line of the country having the longest number of vessels.

3. India is the 20th largest maritime country in the world.

4. India ranks 16th in the world in shipping tonnage.

5. Roughly 95% of the nation's exchange volume (68% as far as worth) is moved via ocean.

6. There are 13 significant ports in the nation separated from around 200 minor ports. Significant ports are under Central Government and others are kept up by State Governments.

Major Ports of the Country

1. Kolkata, 2. Mumbai, 3. Nhava Sheva (J.L. Nehru Port), 4. Tuticorin, 5. Chennai, 6. Mormugao, 7. New Mangalore, 8. Paradeep, 9. Kandla, 10. Vishakhapatnarı, 11. Cochin, 12. Haldia.

Civil Aviation

Air transport began in the nation in 1911. In 1953, as indicated by Air-Corporation Act, all the common flight organizations were nationalized and they went under two new framed partnerships. 1. Indian Airlines (Now Indian) 2. Air India. Indian works inside the nation and neighboring nations while Air India is the national bearer for outer administrations.

Major International Airports :

Delhi (Indira Gandhi International Airport), Mumbai (Santacruz/Sahar) Kolkata Dum Dum), Chennai (Meenambakkam), Amritsar (Raja Sansi) and Trivandrum (Thiruvananthapuram).

PLANNING IN INDIA

The requirement for arranging was felt in India even before independence. A National Planning Committee was set up by the Indian National Congress as right on time as 1938. The Planning Commission was set up in 1950. It is an advisory body occupied with the errand of significant national arranging. The primary goals of India's Economic planning are as per the following: (i) to secure an increase in National Income; (ii) to achieve a planned rate of investment within a given period to bring the actual investment as a proportion of national income to a higher (iii) to reduce inequality in the distribution of income and wealth; (iv) to provide additional employment; (v) to adopt measures to increase agricultural production, manufacturing capacity for producers and a favourable balance of payments.

Five Year Plans in India

Plans	Period	Investment (Rs. Crore)	Objectives
First Plan	April 1, 1951-March 31, 1956	1,960	Focus on agriculture, electricity and irrigation.
Second Plan	April 1, 1956-March 31, 1961	4,672	Focus on basic and heavy industries.
Third Plan	April 1, 1961-March 31, 1966	8,577	Long term development of India's economy
Annual Plan	April 1, 1966-March 31, 1967	2,137	—
Annual Plan	April 1, 1967-March 31, 1968	2,205	—
Annual Plan	April 1, 1968-March 31, 1969	2,283	—
Fourth Plan	April 1, 1969-March 31, 1974	15,779	Increase the income of rural population and supply of goods of mass consumption.
Fifth Plan	April 1, 1974-March 31, 1979	39,426	Self reliance and employment avenues.
Annual Plan	April 1, 1979-March 31, 1980	12,176	—
Sixth Plan	April 1, 1980-	1,09,292	Removal of unemployment.

	March 31, 1985		
Seventh Plan	April 1, 1985- March 31, 1990	2,18,730	Food work and productivity were the basic priorities.
Eighth Plan	April 1, 1992- March 31, 1997	4,95,670	Raising employment.
Ninth Plan	April 1, 1997- March 31, 2002	9,41,041	Agriculture and rural development.
Tenth Plan	April 1, 2002- March 31, 2007	14,91,610	Growth rate 7.8 percent per annum.
Eleventh Paln	April 1, 2007- March 31, 2012	36,44,718	Literacy, employment , rural development and transport deveopment.
Twelfth Plan	April 1, 2012- March 31, 2017	43,30,000	Longterm development of India's economy

Finance Commission

Article 280 of the Constitution accommodates the arrangement of a fund this commission every five year. President appoints chairman and members of this commision. Finance commission commission are to recommend the basis for the distribution of the net proceeds of taxes between the centre and the states and the principles which should govern the grants-in-aid to be given to the states out of the consolidated funds of India.

NITI Aayog

NITI Ayog is framed on the spot of Planning Commission in 2015. It is not a constitutional body. Chairperson of this commission is Prime Minister.

National Development Council

The National Development Council, set-up in 1952, comprises of representatives of the Central Government as well as the State Governments. It is the supreme body in so far as planing is concerned and it determines policies, issues guidelines, reviews working of the plan and finally approves the plan. The Council comprises of the Prime Minister (Chairman), all Union Cabinet Ministers, Chief Ministers all things considered and Union Territories and the Chairman and individuals from the Planning Commission. For issues identifying with Plans and arranging, the Union Minister of Planning is capable to the Parliament.

Stock Exchange

1.Mumbai   2. Chennai 3. Coimbtore 4. Kolkata 5. New Delhi   6. Ahmedabad

7. Vadodara 8. Rajkot 9. Kutch 10. Hyderabad 11. Bengaluru 12. Mangalore

13. Hubli-Dharwar 14. Kochi 15. Bhubaneshwar 16. Jaipur 17. Indore 18. Kanpur

19. Ludhiana 20. Guwahati 21. Magadh (Patna)

All India Services

1. Indian Administrative Services

2. Indian Audit and Accounts Service

3. Indian Foreign Service

4. Indian Forest Service

5. Indian Police Service

6. Indian Postal Service

7. Indian Revenue Service

GENERAL SCIENCE

Branches of Science

Anatomy: The Science dealing with the structure of animals, plants or human body.

Acoustics: The study of sound.

Astrology: The science that deals with the influence of heavenly bodies on human affairs.

Aeronautics: Study of slight.

Chronology: The Science of arran authenticity etc.

Calisthenics: The systematic exercises for attaining strength and gracefulness.

Entomology: The study of insects.

Horticulture: The science dealing with cultivation of flowers, fruits, vegetables and ornamental plants.

Mycology: The study of fungi and fungus diseases.

animals and plants to their surroundings animates and inaniates.

Chronology: The Science arranging time in periods and ascertaining the dates and historical order of past events.

Numismatics: The study of coins gracefulness.

Ceramics: The art and technology of making objects from clay etc (Pottery).

Ornithology: The study of birds.

Philology: The study of written record (any languages) and their authenticity etc.

Philately: The study and collection of postage stamps.

Ecology: The study of the relation of

Phycology: The study of algae.

Toxicology: The study of poisons.

Units

Watts-Power; ohm-Electric resistance; hertz-frequency of wave; bar-Atmospheric Pressure; decibel-Loudness of Sound; Ampere-Electric Current; knot-Speed of Ship; dyne-relative units of force; calorie- Heat; angstrom- Wavelength of light (angle); fathom-Depth of Sea; light year-unit of astronomical distance; carat-Weight of Gold; newton-Force; candela-Luminescence; coulomb-Charge. .

Scientific Instruments

Barometer: Used for measuring atmospheric presssure.

Hygrometer: Used for measuring humidity in air.

Audiometer: Used for measuring intensity of sound.

Odometer: Used in vehicles to measures the distance.

Gyroscope: Used to illustrate dynamics of rotating bodies.

Cardiogram: Used for tracing the movement of heart.

Seismograph: Used for recording the earthquake shocks.

Lactometer: Used for measuring the purity of milk.

Spherometer: Used for measuring curvature of a spherical body.

Sextant: Used for measuring distance of objects.

Radiator: Used in vehicles to provide cooling.

Vitamin & Diet Deficiency

Vitamin	Disease	Sources
Vitamin A	Night Blindness	Carrot, milk, eggs, Papaya
Vitamin B	Beri-Beri	Pulses, eggs, groundnut
Vitamin B2	Cheilosis	Liver, milk, meat
Vitamin B6	Anaemia	Liver, milk, meat
Vitamin B7	Pellagra	Fish, eggs
Vitamin B12	Bloodlessness	Liver, eggs
Vitamin C	Scurvy	Orange, tomato, lemon
Vitamin D	Rickets	Sunlight, eggs, butter, fish oil
Vitamin E	Sterility	Green vegetable, milk, liver
Vitamin K	Delay in Blood Clotting	Green vegetable

Diseases and the Parts of Body they Affect

Disease	Part of body affected	Disease	Part of body affected
AIDS	Immune system of body	Gout	Joints of bone
Arthritis	Inflammation of joints	Jaundice	Liver
Asthma	Lungs	Meningitis	Brain or spinal cord
Cataract	Eyes	Pleurisy	Pleara (inflammation)
Conjunctivitis	Eyes	Polio	Molor neurons
Diabetes	Pancreas	Pneumonia	Lungs
Diphtheria	Throat	Pyorrhoea	Sockets of teeth
Glaucoma	Eyes	Tuberculosis	Lungs
Eczema	Skin	Typhoid	Intestine
Goitre	Front of the neck (due to enlargement of thryroid gland)	Malaria	Spleen

Wellknown Quotations

Swarajya is My Birthright	Bal Gangadhar Tilak
Give me blood, I shall give you freedom	Netajee Subhash Chandra Bose
Inqalab Zindabad	Bhagat Singh
Saare Jahan Se Achcha, Hindustan Hamara	Dr. Mohammed Iqbal
Dilli Chalo	Subhash Chandra Bose
Saffaroshi ki tamanna, Ab Hamare Dil Mein Mai	Ram Prasad Bismil
Agram Haram Hai	Jawar Lal Nehru
Jai Kisan, Jai Kisan, Jai Vigyan	Atal Behari Vajpayee
Speak less, work more	Sanjay Gandhi

I am socialist by nature	Jawahar Lal Nehru
Vijayee Vishwa Tiranga Pyara	Shyam Lal Gupta
Jana Gana Mana Adhinayaka Jai Hail	Rabindranath Tagore
Hate sin, not the sinner	Mahatma Gandhi

ABBREVIATIONS

AAIFR-Appellate Authority for Industrial & Financial Reconstruction

AAAS- American Association of Advancement of Saence

ABC-Atomic, Biological and Chemical (Warfare)

ABM-Anti-Ballistic Missile

ACC-Auxiliary Cadet Corpse

ACD- Asian Co-operation Dialogue

AD- Amo Domini (in the year of Our Lord)

ADB-Asian Development Bank
AEC-Atomic Energy Commission

AFSPA- Armed Forces Special Power Act

AICC-All Inda Congress Committee

AIDS-Acquired Immune Defidency Syndrome

AIMS-All India Management Association

AIML-All India Muslim League

AIMO-All India Manufacturer's Organization

AIIMS-All India Institute of Medical Sciences

AITUC-All India Trade Union Congress

APPLE-Ariane Passenger Payload Experiment

ASEA-Association for South East Asian

ASI-Archaeological Survey of India

ASLV-Augmented Satellite Launch Vehicle

ATN- Asian Television Network

BBC-British Broadcasting Corporation

BC-Before Christ

BHEL-Bharat Heavy Electricals Limited

BIFR-Board of Industrial and financial Reconstruction

BRAI-Broadcast Regulatory Authority of India

BSF-Border Security Force

BSNL-Bharat Sanchar Nigam Limited

CA-Chartered Accountant

CAC- Consumer Access Codes

CBI-Central Bureau of Investigation

CBSE-Central Board of Secondary Education

CBDT-Central Board of Direct Taxes

CDMA-Code Division Multiple Axis

CDRI- Central Drug Research Institute

CHOGM-Commonwealth Heads of Government Meeting

CISF- Central Industrial Security Force

CID-Criminal Investigation Department

CMAG-Commonwealth Ministerial Action Group

COCA - Control of Organised Crime Act

COD-Central Ordinance Depot

CPCB-Central Pollution Control Board

CPI- Communist Party of India

CRPF-Central Reserve Police Force

CRR-Cash Reserve Ratio

CSIR- Council of Scientific & Industrial Research

CVC-Central Vigilance Commission

DGCA-Director General of Civil Aviation

DIG-Deputy Inspector General

DMK-Dravida Munnetra Kazagham

DNA-Deoxyribo Nucleic Acid

BOP-Balance of Payments

ICC-International Cricket Council

ICCRI-Indian Council for Cultural Relations Industrial

ICICI-Industrial Credit and Investment Corporation of India

ICJ-International Court of Justice

ICMR-Indian Council of Medical Research

ICS-Indian Civil Service

ICWA-Indian Council of World Affairs

IDA-International Development Agency

IDBA-Industrial Development Bank of India

IFFI-International Film Festival of India

IFS-Indian Foreign Service

IGNOU-Indira Gandhi National Open University

IIT-Indian Institute of Technology

ILO-International Labour Organisation

IMF-International Monetary Fund

INTERPOL-International Police Organisation

IOC-Indian Oil Corporation

IPC-Indian Penal Code

IPCL-Indian Petro-Chemicals Corporation Ltd

ISD-International Subscriber Dialing

ISRO-Indian Space Research Organisation

IST-Indian Standard Institution

IST-Indian Standard Time

ITO-International Trade Organisation

ITC-International Tele-communication

ITUC-Indian Trade Union Congress

GSC-Global System for Communication

HAL-Hindustan Aeronautics Limited

HDC-Hill Development Council

HEC-Heavy Engineering Corporation

HMT-Hindustan Machine Tools

IAA-International Airports Authority

IAF-Indian Air Force

IARI-Indian Agricultural Research Institute

IAS-Indian Administrative Service

IAAS-Indian Audit and Accounts Service

IATA-International Air Transport Association

IBM-International Business Machines

ISRO-Indian Space Research Organisation

ISI-Indian Standard Institution

IST-Indian Standard Time

ITI-Indian Telephone Industries

ITO-International Trade Organisation

ITU-International Telecommunication Union

ITUC-Indian Trade Union Congress

ICAR-Indian Council of Agricultural Research
EAS-East Asia Summit
ECA-Economic Cooperation Administration

ECG-Electro Cardiogram

ECO-Economic Cooperation Organisation

EEC-European Economic Commission

EMS-European Monetary System

ESI-Employees State Insurance

ESRO-European Space Research Organisation

FAO-Food and Agriculture Organisation

JCO-Junior Commissioned Officer

JMM-Jharkhand Mukti Morcha

JPC-Joint Parliamentary Committee

LASER-Light Amplification by Stimulated Emmission of Radiation

LCA-Light Combat Aircraft

LIC-Life Insurance Corporation

LPG-Liquified Petroleum Gas

FBI-Federal Bureau of Investigation
FERA-Foreign Exchange Regulation Act
FARB-Foreign Exchange Regulatory Board

GAIL-Gas Authority of India Limited

GATT-General Agreement on Tariffs and Trade
GMT-Greenwich Mean Time

GNP-Gross National Product

GPRS-General Packet Radio Service

GSLV-Geo-Satellite Launch Vehicle

SAARC-South Asian Association for Regional Corporation

SAHR-South Asian for Human Rights

SC-Supreme Court
SEBI-Securities and Exchange Board of India
SEZ-Special Economic Zone
SHO-Station House Officer
SIM-Subscriber Identification Module
MLA-Member of Legislative Assembly
MI-Military Intelligence
MBA-Master of Business Administration

MODVAT-Modified Value Added Tax
NABARD-National Bank for Agriculture and Rural Development
NASA-National Aeronautics and Space Admintration
NATO-North Atlantic Treaty Organisation
NCC-National Cadet Corp

NCER-National Council of Educational Research

NDA-National Defence Academy

NHAI-National Highway Authority of India
NHRC-National Human Rights Commission
TRAI-Telecom Regulatory Authority of India
PA-Personal Assistant, Press Association
PAN-Permanent Account Number
PIO-Persons of Indian Origin
POTA-Prevention of Terrorism Act
OMG-Quarter Master General
OMT-Quantitative Management Technique
RDR-Radio Detecting and Ranging

RAF-Rapid Action Force

RAW-Research & Analysis Wing

OCS-Overseas Communication Service

OPEC-Organisation of Petroleum Exporting Countries

RCC-Reinforced Cement Concrete

RSP-Rourkela Steel Plant

RBI-Reserve Bank of India

UTI-Unit Trust of India

UNESCO-United Nations Educational Scientific and Cultural Organisation

UNIEF-United Nations International Emergency Fund

UNFCCC-United Nations Framework Convention Climate Change

WEF-World Environment Forum

wef-with effect from

WHO-World Health Organisation

WFP-World Food Programme

WWF-Wortd WildLife Fund

WTO-World Trade Organisation

VAT-Value Added Tax

VIP-Very Important Person

Books and Authors

Authors Name	Book Name
Margaret Atwood	The Testaments
Richard Powers	The Overstory
PM Narendra Modi	The Braille edition of the book Exam Warriors
Viswanathan Anand and Susan Ninan	Mind-Master
Ranjan Gogoi	"Courts of India"
Neha J Hiranandani	Girl Power: Indian Women Who Broke The Rules
Vikram Sampath	Savarkar: Echoes from a forgotten past, 1883-1924
Peter Baker	Obama: The Call of History
Adi Shankaracharya	Vivekadeepini
M Venkaiah Naidu	Listening, Learning and Leading
Meenakshi Lekhi	'The New Delhi Conspiracy'
Dr. A.P.J. Abdul Kalam	My Journey
Dr. Bibek Debroy	Making of New India
Dr. Krishna Saksena	"Whispers of Time"
Dr. Y.V. Reddy	Indian Fiscal Federalism
Malala Yousafzai	We are Displaced
R Uma Maheswari	From Possession to Freedom
Raghuram Rajan	The Third Pillar
Ruchir Sharma	'Undaunted: Saving the Idea of India'
Shahid Afridi	Game Changer
Changing India	Dr. Manmohan Singh
Maharana Pratap: The Invincible Warrior	Rima Hooja

Making of Legend	Bindeshwar Pathak
Diabetes with Delight	Anoop Misra
Indian Cultures as Heritage	Romila Thapar
Matoshree	Sumitra Mahajan
The Coalition years	Pranab Mukherjee
Fire and Fury: Inside the Trump Whitehouse	Michael Wolff
Citizen Delhi: My Times, My Life	Sheila Dikshit
Mere Sapno Ka Bharat	Tarun Vijay
A World of Three Zeroes: The New Economics of Zero Poverty, Zero Unemployment, and Zero Carbon Emission	Mohammad Yunus
Hit Refresh	Satya Nadella
Imperfect (autobiography)	Sanjay Manjrekar
Immortal India	Amish Tripathi
Two	Gulzar
What happened	Hilary Clinton
Why I am hindu	Shashi Tharoor
Indira Gandhi: A Life in Nature	Jairam Ramesh
Enemies and Neighbours: Arabs and Jews in Palestine and Israel, 1917-2017	Ian Black
I do what I do	Raghuram Rajan
Indian Political Theory: Laying the Ground work for Swaraj	Aakash Singh Rathore
Stalin: Waiting for Hitler 1928-1941	Stephen Kotkin
281 and Beyond	V V S Laksman
Moments ofTruth: My Life with Acting	Roshan Taneja
Where India Goes	Diane Coffey and Dean Spears
A Tale of Two Victoria Crosses	Lt Gen Baljit Singh
No Room for Small Dreams	Shimon Peres
Democracy's XI: The Great Indian Cricket Story	Rajdeep Sardesai
A Republic in the Making: India in the 1950s	Gyanesh Kudaisya

India Turns East: International Engagement and US-China Rivalry	Fredrick Grare
The Ministry of Utmost Happiness	Arundhati Roy
China & India War: Collision Course on the Roof of the World	Bertil Lintner
Unstoppable: My Life So Far	Maria Sharapova
Conflict of Interest	Sunita Narain
Atal Ji Ne kaha	Birendra Rehi
No Spin	Shane Warne
Gorbachev: His Life and Times	William Taubman
Evolution	Emmanuel Macron
Reimagining Pakistan	Husain Haggani
Reporting Pakistan	Meena Menon
A Century Is Not Enough	Sourav Ganguly
The Perils of Being Moderately Famous	Soha Ali Khan
Triple Talaq: Examining Faith	Salman Khurshid
Kashmir: Exploring the Myth Behind the Narrative	Khalid Bashir
The Only Story	Julian Barnes
An Uncertain Glory: India and Its Contradiction	Amartya Sen and Jean Dreze
In a Free State	VS Naipaul
Straight Talk	Abhishek Manu Singhvi
The President Is Missing	Bill Clinton and James Patterson
Syama Prasad Mookerjee: Life and Times	Tathagata Roy
Gandhi: The Years That Changed the World (1914-1948)	Ramachandra Guha

COMPUTER AWARENESS

Introduction

This is the period of data innovation. We will undoubtedly observe a Computer upset in which information handling and recovery are being wear dependably at inconceivable velocities. Today Computer are to be found in each of life. This supernatural gadget would be able to be found in children's toys, word processors, pocket calculators, industrial robots, home appliances etc., to mention few of their innumerable uses; and there practically no new machine, instrument, control equipment or information system that does not have a microprocessor in it. The new generation Computer has just entered its fifth era. The initial four ages of Computer being founded on the innovation of the age to which they had a place.

Background

In the event that we search for the beginning of the most progressive creation of the advanced age, known as Computer, at that point we would ave to return to seventeenth century. Strikingly, the roots of the mechanical computerized number crunchers can be followed to the mathematicians Blaise Pascal (1623-62) and Gotffried Wilhelm Liebnitz (16461716). Charles Babbage (1792-1871) was the first to think about a machine to deliver and store the tables of logarithms developed by John Napier(1550-1617).

Electronic Brains

The modern computers are able to do such fantastics accomplishments that these have been named as electronic brains, however these can not been called insightful in the human sense. Their minds are not fit for adopting the thought process of a human brain. Actually, these refined machines can just do what they are instructed to.

The Digital Computer

Most common among the computers, the digital computers, are all inclusive as in these have applications not only in the logical field yet in addition in the fields of business and organization. In fact, due to their flexibility and accuracy, today, the digital computers dominate the scene. The latest of these computers are called microcomputers which are handy and user-friendly.

The First Computer

In February 1946, the world's first allelectronic digital computer, called ENIAC, the Electronic Numerical Integator And Calculator, was officially devoted. This was the first generation computer based on vacuum tube technology. In June 1945, John Von Neumann, an extraordinary mathematician and rationalist, arranged the "primary draft of a Report on the EDVAC" (Electronic Discrete Variable Automatic Computer). The Von Neumann configuration depended on a solitary Central Processor Unit (CPU) pérforming successive procedure on an arranged grouping of directions, called a program, to create the ideal outcome.

Operation

Number Crunching: Prior, figuring the finance of a huge organization required a large number of arithmetical computations, yet today, it very well may be finished by a central computer because manipulating numbers-number crunching is what a computer does in a best manner.

Data Processing : As an information the computer shows another quality. Experts feed the data (information) into it as figures.This is called data processing.

Binary System: Zeros and ones, in their endless combinations constitute binary system on which computer operation is based. Under the binary system all ordinary arithmetical operations are reduced to their simplest form.

Hardware and Software

A computer system is commonly viewed as made oftwo parts—the hardware and the software. The hardware comprises of the physical pieces of the machine. The software comprises of the data and the guidelines given the computer that empower it to work. The information is called data and the Of instructions,is called program.

Programming

Programming is the name given to 'craft' of composing a program. Each machine, contingent on its internal hardware architecture, has a special level language called the machine language. In a binary-coded digital computer, the machine language is comprised of 0s and 1s. Assembly Language utilizes amemonics for machine language . To diminish the programer from the distress of a program in the the difficult lowlevel machine language, a few several simpler, high-level programming languages have been created. High level languages are fathomable portrayals of machine code utilizing mneplonics in Assembly Language.

Languages: Computer programming, languages are frequently recognized as being either ordered or deciphered languages. The user's program in the high-level programming language is called the source code. "The producer 'Of the Computer supplies the necessary programming, either a compiler or an interpreter, for each client language actualized on it. The complier makes an interpretation of the source code into a machine language program called the object code.

Different Computers

Today computers can be named Mainframe Computers, Minicomputers; and Microcomputers. Mainframe Computers are costly ahd huge with unified figuring offices where Super Computer or a large computer is associated with a few terminals. A multi user mainframe computer has a large memory and is capable of speeds of the order of several millions of floating-point operations per second. Minicomputers are also multi-user computers having lesser memory and operate at slower speeds.

Desk Top System: The fourth generation micro computer like the is a small with two floppy disk drives. It utilizes a multiprocessor and has a RAM, five expansion slots and functions under the System called MS-DOS.

The Floppy Disk: The most broadly acknowledged type of auxiliary storage utilized in microcomputers is the floppy disk storage. A floppy diskette is a round vinyl circle encased inside aplastic cover.

Hard Disk : The hard disk drives can store considerably more information than what can be put away on a floppy Hard disks come fixed and they can't be expelled or changed like floppy diskettes.

The Operating System: The Operating System of a computer is group of programs that manages or oversees all the operations of the Computer such as CPU, Memory, Keyboard, Hoppy Diskette, VDU etc. The operating system is responsible for the files on the disk and the communication between the computer and its peripherals.

Commands: All operating systems have inbuilt and small programs residing on disk which, when run, behave like commands.

Printer: The printer usally utilized alongside a microcomputer is a dot matrix printer, wherein a 9 pin (vertical) head makes matrix pattern to form the characters. Be that as it may, these days, laser printers are more stylish. A Laser (LASER:Light Amplification by Emission of Radiation) is gadget that harmness light produce an intense beam of radiation of a very pure and single colour.

Information Technology (IT): Today, computers are assuming an ever-expanding job during the time spent improving the progression of data among individuals and machines. This is a field which is presently known as Information Technology (IT).

Network: A network is the means which computers share and exchange information and resources across eith short distances (LAN Local Area Networks) or globally (WAN : Wide Area Networks). Today , networking system is useful in utilizing business assets, upgrading profitability and proficiency, and diminishing expense.

Printed in Great Britain
by Amazon

13611361R00058